NISSAN SKYLINE
GT-R

1989 | *Limited Edition Extra* | 2002

Compiled by
R.M.Clarke

ISBN 1 85520 634X

BROOKLANDS BOOKS LTD.
P.O. BOX 146, COBHAM,
SURREY, KT11 1LG. UK
sales@brooklands-books.com

www.brooklands-books.com

Printed in China

ACKNOWLEDGEMENTS

The Skyline isn't a car that one sees everyday and its background is even more obscure. Classic Cars in the final article in this book expertly traces its heritage and sets the scene for the introduction of the GT-R in 1989.

"There's been a Skyline in Nissan's line-up since Nissan merged with fellow Japanese manufacturer Prince in 1966. But the Skyline itself goes back to 1957, and its competition history to 1965, when Prince first entered the car in Japanese saloon car racing. Says Nigel Gates, Skyline expert at the Datsun Owners' Club: 'The mid-Sixties Skyline GT-A and GT-B have the sort of respect in Japan that the Lotus Cortina has in Britain. Prince was a very technically-minded company, and Nissan kept its spirit alive with the Skyline. 'In 1969, the third generation Skyline arrived, and with it the GT-R badge. That car dominated Japanese saloon car racing before Mazda came along with the RX-3. It had a 2.0-litre, twin-cam, 24-valve, triple-carb straight six, good for 160bhp. Good short-wheelbase coupe versions fetch £20,000 in Japan.' With the fourth generation in 1972, the GT-R became more of a road car; the fuel crisis put paid to the GT-R in 1977. Nissan's philosophy had changed, and the big Skyline coupe became more of a luxury cruiser. It found its sporting feet again in 1981, with the 190bhp four-cylinder R30 RS Turbo, and in 1986, the R31 GTS-X went back to the Skyline's twin-cam six-cylinder roots but provided a foretaste of the R32, with fourwheel steering. Says Nigel: 'Nissan got the taste for racing again, and laid down the gauntlet in the technology stakes. When the R32 revived the GT-R name in 1989, it was so far ahead of its time that they've hardly altered it since."

For more than 40 years, Brooklands Books have been publishing compilations of road tests and other articles from the English speaking world's leading motoring magazines. We have already produced more than 700 titles, and in these we have made available to motoring enthusiasts some 25,000 stories which would otherwise have become hard to find. For the most part, our books focus on a single model, and as such they have become an invaluable source of information. As Bill Boddy of *Motor Sport* was kind enough to write when reviewing one of our Gold Portfolio volumes, "the Brooklands catalogue must now constitute the most complete historical source of reference available, at least of the more recent makes and models."

Even so, we are constantly being asked to publish new titles on cars which have a narrower appeal than those we have already covered in our main series. The economics of book production make it impossible to cover these subjects in our main series, but Limited Edition and Limited Edition Extra volumes, like this one, give us a way to tackle these less popular but no less worthy subjects.

Both the Limited Edition and Limited Edition Extra series maintain the same high standards of presentation and reproduction set by our established ranges. However, each volume is printed in smaller quantities - which is perhaps the best reason we can think of as to why you should buy this book now. We would also like to remind readers that we are always open to suggestions for new titles; perhaps your club or interest group would like us to consider a book on your particular subject?

Finally, we are more than pleased to acknowledge that Brooklands Books rely on the help and co-operation of those who publish the magazines where the articles in our books originally appeared. For this present volume, we gratefully acknowledge the continued support of the publishers of *Autocar, Automobile Magazine, Car, Car and Driver, Cars & Car Conversions, Classic Cars, Motor Australia, Performance Car, EVO, Sports Car International, Top Gear* and *Wheels* for allowing us to include their valuable and informative copyright stories.

R.M. Clarke.

CONTENTS

4	High-Tech Skyline Causes a Sensation	*Autocar*	July 5	1989
6	Sky's the Limit	*Motor Australia*	Aug	1989
12	The World's most Advanced Road Car	*Car*	Feb	1990
16	The Nissan that Leaves the Sierra Cosworth Standing	*Autocar*	Nov 28	1990
20	Godzilla! - Competition	*Sports Car International*	Mar	1991
24	Blood Sports - Drive Report	*Wheels*	May	1991
28	Blown Chances - Nissan Skyline GT-R V-spec vs. Toyota Supra Comparison Test	*Motor Australia*	Sept	1993
36	Killer Godzilla!	*Wheels*	Mar	1995
42	Famous Skyline Track Test	*Sports Car International*	Sept	1995
44	Ode to a Skyline Road Test	*Car and Driver*	Dec	1995
50	Reach for the Skyline - Comparison Test	*Performance Car*	Sept	1997
58	Nissan Skyline Road Test	*Autocar*	Oct 15	1997
64	Hard Rock vs. New Wave - Skyline GT-R vs. Lotus Esprit V8 GT Comparison Test	*Top Gear*	July	1998
70	Big Boy's Toys Drive Report	*Cars & Car Conversions*	Apr	1999
75	Sky's the Limit	*Top Gear*	Apr	1999
76	V-Special Drive Report	*Autocar*	Apr 28	1999
84	Skyline's New Limit	*Wheels*	Apr	1999
90	Yum and Yummer - Nissan Skyline GT-R vs. Mitsubishi EVO VI Comparison Test	*Autocar*	Aug 11	1999
98	Reach for the Skyline Long Term Test	*Autocar*	Dec 8	1999
101	Nissan Skyline GT-R	*Automobile Magazine*	May	1999
102	Sky Larks Long Term Test	*Top Gear*	Feb	2000
108	Sushi Quattro - Nissan Skyline GT-R vs. Audi RS4 Comparison Test	*Car*	July	2000
114	Skyline R33 GT-R Used Car of the Month	*Top Gear*	Aug	2000
116	Coogan's Runabout Long Term Report	*Car*	Aug	2000
120	Nissan Skyline GT-R M-spec Driven	*EVO*	Sept	2001
122	Setting Sons - R32 - R33 - R34	*EVO*	Mar	2002
126	The Fast & the Furious - Nissan Skyline GT-R vs. Honda NSX Comparison Test	*Autocar*	Apr 3	2002
132	Reach for the Sky - 1992 R32 Skyline GT-R	*Classic Cars*	June	2001

High-tech Skyline causes a sensation

Until Nissan's spectacular state-of-the-art Skyline GT-R arrives, the four-wheel-steer GTS-t is the next best thing. Peter Nunn reckons it's a worthy substitute

NISSAN'S LAUNCH OF THE muscular new Skyline marks the comeback of a true Japanese legend.

There have been Skylines since 1955 (although not in the UK) but none to compare with this spectacular, eighth generation version, which gets new engines, bodies and interiors and embraces the very latest in Nissan chassis technology.

Think of a Sierra Cosworth or, even better, a 3-litre Capri, 15-20 years on — completely revamped with hi-tech suspension, turbo engine, new body and so on, but still with that same, earthy boy racer appeal — and you're getting close to what the Skyline's all about.

Unquestionably, the highlight is the formidable new Skyline GT-R, with twin turbo 280bhp engine, all-new multi-link suspension, with computerised, variable torque-split four-wheel-drive and the latest HICAS four-wheel-steering. It's an amazing car, but until it hits the streets this August, the hottest Skyline is this GTS-t. Its Type M equipment package gives it a lot of what the GT-R has to offer for around half the price.

With rear-drive and smaller 1998cc engine, the GTS might seem an anticlimax to the GT-R. On the contrary, its six-cylinder, twin-cam 24-valve turbo engine makes it monstrously fast. A test GTS recently burned from 0-60mph in just 6.8secs in the hands of Japan's *Car Graphic* magazine, while superb chassis control makes it possibly the best handling car yet to come out of Japan. It's easy to see what all the fuss is about.

The GTS's RB 20 DETT engine (which also features in the Laurel and Cefiro saloons) makes evocative, BMW-type straight six noises at low speeds and, thanks to a new, low friction roller bearing turbo with intercooler, should be quick and free from the dreaded lag.

Unfortunately, this powerful engine, which provides such blistering mid and top-end pace, is woefully slow at the bottom end — below 3000rpm, there's nothing. But the trade-off is a boost which comes in smoothly as the engine (leisurely) gathers pace, pulling from, say, 1000rpm in fourth without protest.

Though the engine spins easily and, on the motorway, the Skyline will surge ahead with just the slightest movement of the accelerator, its infectious smoothness disappears beyond 4000rpm, making the last few 1000rpm up to the 7500rpm red line not quite so easy on the ears. It's not harsh, just fussy.

Still, in the eye of the enthusiast, the sheer power — all 215bhp of it at 6400rpm, with torque of 195lb ft peaking at 3200rpm — not to mention the daunting acceleration and 130mph+ speeds of which the GTS is surely capable, are the things that matter most.

The Skyline is one heavyweight performer, a car with Sierra dimensions but Granada bulk. Weighing in at 2778lb it stands 178ins long, 66.7ins wide and 52.5ins tall. Its saloon cousin, 2ins longer and fractionally lower, shares the same 102.9ins wheelbase.

Neither knocks you down with lines of outlandish beauty (as does the new Nissan 200 SX), yet the rather conservative lines quickly grow on you. The Skyline has presence.

Fittingly, the GTS has a chassis to cope with the new order of Skylines — and this is world-class. It comes wholesale from the new 300 ZX: new generation, coil-sprung multi-link axles appear front and rear, backed up by Nissan's new SUPER-HICAS 4ws. Tyres are 205/55 R16 88Vs.

Six-cylinder twin cam 24-valve turbo gives GTS daunting acceleration — 0-60mph in just 6.8secs. Steering wheel is big and business-like but fussy switchgear spoils facia

Computerised 4wd from the GT-R is available, too, but not in Type M spec shown here which gives special wheels and tyres, extra equipment plus that neat boot spoiler.

Even before you move off, the solid, no-nonsense message of the Skyline comes across loud and clear. There's a big, business-like three-spoke wheel to guide the beast, matched to speed-sensing steering with electronic control, giving 2.6 turns lock to lock.

To the left, a meaty manual shift is standard. Though no flick-switch

device, it's still quick and easy between ratios and feels good. Pedals are well arranged and the big seats support in all the right places.

The interior is new, comfortably furnished and, at a pinch, can seat four, although rear legroom isn't that generous. The sloping centre console has hints of 928 about it, and while the facia is clear, it's spoilt by fussy switchgear of the type Citroen discarded years ago. It does all work, but visually it's a mess. The plasticky finish of the various dash mouldings

Even on fast bends, GTS turns in beautifully. Rear wheels can be leant on to power through corners, the multi-link geometry curbing lift-off oversteer

and wheel disappoints, too, especially after the success of the 200 SX.

As you get under way, disappointment quickly vanishes. Right from the start, you can tell this Skyline is something special — and on Japanese roads, you can't even scratch the surface of what it can really do.

In a straight line, the GTS is both fast and stable, using a viscous coupling to help put the power down. But there's refinement too; the car cruises quietly and easily, with little wind or mechanical noise.

As the pace quickens, you can feel the steering stiffen, but still the action is fluid, responsive. The car enters low speed corners in an entirely flat, neutral fashion, the taut suspension keeping the ride firm.

On faster bends the picture's much the same: the GTS still turns in beautifully but there's a trace of understeer and a few extra degrees of roll. Keep the power on and the Skyline still holds its line. But if the corner's tight enough, the tail might be persuaded out into a delicious, elegant slide, which can then be held simply with a dab of opposite lock.

This is great fun. You can really lean on those rear wheels to power you through the corner, the multilink

geometry doing an effective job of curbing any hint of lift-off oversteer, the Bridgestone RE 71s providing high levels of grip.

Contributing to all this is the new SUPER-HICAS 4ws, which initially turns the rear wheels in the opposite direction to the fronts (up to a maximum 1-deg), before switching to parallel steer.

The system is speed-sensitive, reacting to vehicle speed, acceleration, plus the speed and angle through which you turn the wheel. But you don't notice it — the Skyline feels totally natural and wieldy, exhibiting none of the nervousness of some other 4ws systems.

Powerful all-ventilated discs, matched to aluminium four piston calipers and ABS are also part of this accomplished Skyline chassis and these provide effortless stopping power without fade.

Perhaps the most staggering part comes at the end. For in Japan, the price for all this is little more than that of an XR3i in the UK — a fully-loaded GTS retails for just £10,647.

Unfortunately, there are no export plans, for this Skyline GTS must rank not only as a bargain, but also as a great driving machine. ∎

SPECIFICATION

ENGINE
Longways, front. **Capacity** 1998cc, 6 cylinders in line.
Bore 78.0mm, **stroke** 69.7mm.
Compression ratio 8.5:1.
Head/block alloy/iron.
Valve gear dohc, 4 valves per cylinder.
Ignition and fuel Single ceramic turbo with intercooler, ECCS programmed fuel injection and ignition.
Max power 215bhp (PS-JIS) (158kW ISO) at 6400rpm. **Max torque** 195lb ft (262 Nm) at 3200rpm.

TRANSMISSION
Rear-drive. 5-speed manual.

Gear	Ratio
Top	0.759
4th	1.000
3rd	1.308
2nd	1.902
1st	3.321
Final drive	4.363

SUSPENSION
Front, independent, multilink axle (lower arms, upper curved links, tie-rods, coil springs/damper units, anti-roll bar).
Rear, independent, multilink axle (lower wishbones, multiple upper arms, coil springs/damper units, anti-roll bar).

STEERING
Rack and pinion, speed-sensing assistance.

BRAKES
Front Ventilated discs **Rear** Ventilated discs. (Optional ABS). Vacuum servo.

TYRES
205/55 R16 88V.

DIMENSIONS

	Coupe	Saloon
Length	178.3ins	180.3ins
Width	66.7ins	66.7ins
Height	52.2ins	52.2ins
Wheelbase	102.9ins	102.9ins
Kerb weight	2778-2822lb	2844-2888lb

Sky's the limit

Nissan's new Skyline GT-R is techno to the hilt.

by Peter Lyon

There's a new catchphrase being bandied around the boardrooms of Nissan's Tokyo-based headquarters these days and it's all part of a new thrust by the company to be at the forefront of automotive technology by the start of the nineties. Called "Project 901" — for "nineties-number one" — the phrase denotes a body of design ideas behind Nissan's drive to displace Honda as Japan's most advanced car manufacturer. The new Skyline range, including the fire-breathing hi-tech GT-R version, as revealed exclusively in last month's Modern MOTOR, is the spearhead.

Technically speaking Nissan has for years been regarded as the poorer son of the four big Japanese manufacturers (Honda, Toyota, Mazda, Nissan) but a rapid-fire model rejuvenation, with the new 300ZX, Maxima and Infiniti ranges, has seen the aspirations of the company, like its rising sun emblem, elevate to new heights.

Young Japanese automotive graduates now consider Nissan the up-and-coming force, as opposed to the previously popula Honda, and are virtually queuing at th door of the company's Atsugi Technica Centre for a chance to work on the 90 project.

We at Modern MOTOR had an inklin something very special was in the pipelin when Editor, Barry Lake, was presente with a wry smile by the company's numbe one Australian driver, Jim Richards, as a answer to future model expectations What we didn't count on though was th advanced state of the company's vast arra

6

The car to put Nissan among Japan's top hi-tech manufacturers, the Skyline GT-R. The sights are set on Group A dominance.

...f technological nous — the new GT-R is ...y far the most advanced touring car to ...ome out of Japan.

Unlike previous Skyline models this car ...s of a completely new design. Gone is the ...rchaic square-edged styling and in its ...lace is a svelte and attractive car that out-...ardly appears European. It also packs ...nough technological muscle to make even ...he biggest Japanese sumo wrestler run for ...over.

Although most of the kudos for the new ...kyline will fall well and truly upon the

top-of-the-range GT-R there are, al-together, 13 different models in the new line-up. They range from a basic 1.8-litre four-cylinder producing 68 kW through to a potent 4wd 160 kW 2.0-litre in-line six that employs a new roller-bearing tur-bocharger claimed to reduce friction by up to 60 per cent.

While some may marvel at the myriad of technological features incorporated on the GT-R, especially the chassis and drive train, it's the engine that provides the im-petus for the whole car.

The new 2.6-litre engine (codenamed RB 26 DETT) is based on the familiar in-line six-cylinder block fitted to the current 3.0-litre Skyline and once used by Holden in the 3.0-litre turbocharged VL Com-modore. Twin belt-driven camshafts sit astride the engine operating a 24-valve head while two ceramic Garrett tur-bochargers together with intercoolers as well as an advanced electronics package, controlling both injection and ignition, round out what can only be described as an extremely potent and purposeful race-bred powerplant.

Nissan has come tantalisingly close to the benchmark 223 kW (300 bhp) figure with power and torque outputs quoted at 211 kW (280 bhp) at 6800 rpm and 353 Nm at 4400 rpm respectively.

There are suggestions engineers toyed

with the idea of "dialling" in extra horse-power by increasing the turbo boost pres-sure but discussions among prominent Japanese automotive authorities regard-ing excessive power outputs in relation to environmental issues halted it.

Understandably Nissan has chosen to keep tightlipped about performance figures for the GT-R except the basic 0-100 km/h and standing 400 metres which together reflect the effectiveness of the car's incredibly high power output as well as its ability to transfer it to the bitumen.

From a standing start the GT-R sizzles to 100 km/h in just 5.03 seconds and there-after it doesn't let up: 400 metres is covered in an amazing 13.47 seconds.

These times compare more than favourably against its two most highly rated Group A competitors, namely Ford and Holden. Ford's all-conquering Sierra RS500 returns 6.40 sec and 14.70 sec respectively for the same tests, while Holden's Group A VL Commodore tends to look somewhat staid at 7.04 sec and 15.22 sec. It must be said, though, that manufacturer's claims are often hard to duplicate.

All that performance takes a power of stopping when required. Nissan has taken no risks by fitting the GT-R with a for-midable anti-lock braking system that on paper looks more likely to appear on a European supercar. Massive, aluminium four-piston 296 mm by 30.5 mm ventilated discs sit up front while the rear end gets a

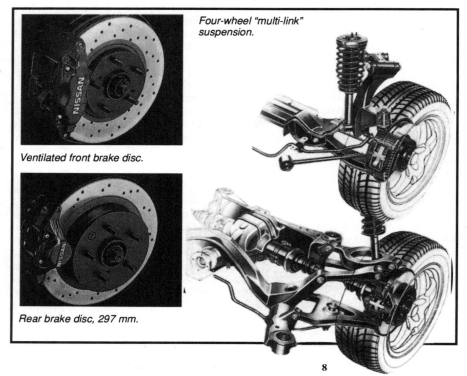

The ATTESA ETS 4wd system is unique in using an accelerometer to measure sideways forces and adjust the torque split accordingly.

Four-wheel "multi-link" suspension.

Ventilated front brake disc.

Rear brake disc, 297 mm.

The new 2.6-litre engine is based on the six cylinder block fitted to the current Skyline, but boasts Garrett turbochargers and 24 valves. Claimed output is 211 kW at 6800 rpm.

two-piston 297 mm by 18 mm variety.

With such a lofty power output in road going form, it was essential to engineer a transmission and drive train set-up that could handle the quoted power output of 410 kW (550 bhp) at 7600 rpm which the car is said to be developing in Group A trim.

And that Nissan has. It's called AT-TESA ETS or, for the techno minded, Advanced Total Traction Engineering System for All terrains and Electronic Torque Split. It is unique among production four-wheel drive systems as it employs an accelerometer to detect lateral or sideways movements and adjusts the torque split (power) accordingly to each wheel. Other manufacturers are known to be working on such systems but Nissan is the only company confident enough to put one into production.

Put simply the ATTESA ETS system consists of a computer controlled multi-plate clutch encased in oil as well as a hydraulic unit triggered by changes in the speed sensors and accelerometer, which applies pressure to the clutch to vary torque split.

Driving through a Trojan-like five-speed gearbox and limited-slip differential, the hydraulic unit reduces torque to the front wheels as lateral movement is increased, thus combining the cornering characteristics of a conventional rear-wheel drive set-up together with the sure-footed traction provided by four-wheel drive.

One thing we must dispute though is Nissan's claim that ATTESA ETS is the

irst 4wd system to be combined with anti-lock braking. Lancia has been developing such a system for a number of years now and recently unveiled a production version on its new 16-valve Delta Integrale.

Nissan obviously considers its new AT-TESA ETS system is ready to withstand the enormous stresses encountered during the rigors of competitive Group A motor racing. This is certainly not the first time 4wd has been considered for the race track: Lotus once raced an all-wheel drive car in Formula One, but in recent times weight has prohibited manufacturers from even contemplating such a move. Our bet is that, rule book permitting, Nissan will develop the ATTESA ETS system for fitment on its potent Group C sportscar challenger which recently qualified in 12th position at the Le Mans 24 hour race.

The new Skyline's suspension also sets new standards for Nissan. The car is fitted with the company's recently developed multi-link suspension set-up which first appeared on the new 300ZX. Its history has a novel twist in that its design was spawned out of an ideas basket initiated by the company's 901 chassis-development leader, Takaaki Uno, who took aside his engineers and asked them to generate at least 100 new design proposals for future models.

A number of front-end multi-link set-ups were tested before a final production version was chosen using a lateral link, a trailing strut and a diagonal upper control link which locates the steering knuckle on each side of the car.

It's obvious Nissan's engineers had a long hard look at other manufacturers' set-ups and while some may regard the Skyline's front suspension as revolutionary it is in essence a sophisticated version of the tried and proven independent set-up that utilises unequal length upper and lower control arms. It is also strikingly similar to the system used by Honda except that it employs one extra link between the knuckle and the upper locating link.

From the ground up the GT-R exudes aggressiveness and this is nowhere more evident than the rubber with which the car is shod. Meaty 225/50 R16 92V Bridgestone RE71 Potenza radials sit upon equally purposeful 8JJ X 16 alloy wheels providing the sort of grip and traction a car with 211 kW on tap requires. The five-spoke wheel design supplies substantial airflow to the braking system and blends well with the car's styling.

Similarly interesting as the new AT-TESA ETS 4wd is Nissan's new Super HICAS four-wheel steering system — another Skyline GT-R first.

The 4ws system employed on the GT-R is a third generation version of the original Super HICAS system. Whereas the older system was often criticised for its ungainly low-speed manoeuvrability, the new Super HICAS does away with that by initially turning the rear wheels in the opposite direction to those at the front before switching back the other way to run in unison. This, says Nissan, improves low-down steering responsiveness and feel while still maintaining the useful gains during high-speed cornering. While it is in effect similar to Honda's patented 4ws system its operation is by hydraulic pressure, depending upon speed and angle, as opposed to conventional mechanical gears.

In a racing environment the Super HICAS 4ws system, together with the GT-R's power-assisted rack and pinion steering, should prove most useful on tight and twisty circuits where cornering speeds, as opposed to outright top-end speed, come into play. Those lucky enough to have driven the GT-R say its the best handling car to come out of Japan — high praise when you consider the numerous models the country pumps out each year. Four-wheel steering is still an unknown quantity on the race track but from our experience, given the right circumstances, it should perform well.

With such impressive mechanical credentials the Skyline's body stylists certainly had the job before them especially when you consider the two varying functions the car is expected to perform. On one hand it must act as a slightly upmarket family-orientated sedan while on the other it must fulfil the role of an all-conquering race car.

As with Nissan's engineers, the stylists have risen to the task well and sculpted an extremely attractive package. There's no doubting, the curvaceous but aggressive styling is definitely a winner. Sure there's nothing to stamp the styling as revolutionary but the addition of rear-wheel arch blisters, side-skirting, a large front air dam and a high boot mounted spoiler combine to make the GT-R one of the most attractive while at the same time purposeful cars to come out of Japan.

But attractiveness doesn't always augur well in the aerodynamics department! The GT-R's rather "clumsy" 0.40 C_d atests to that and, together with the car's hefty kerb weight of 1430 kg, must pose at least a few problems for the engineers at NISMO (Nissan's racing department) whose job it is to develop the car into a lean and mean winning machine. For weight saving purposes Nissan has fitted an aluminium bonnet and front panels. But with such extensive chassis mechanicals the GT-R was always going to be a heavyweight. For comparison, the Sierra RS500 and Group A Commodore tip the scales at 1240 kg and 1410 kg respectively.

Much of the GT-R's poor aerodynamics can be contributed to the wide Bridgestone RE71 Potenza tyres as well as the added aerodynamic aids which, on the race track, are necessary to provide optimal downforce for high-speed stability. The more sedate two and four-door Skylines vary from a respectable 0.31 through to 0.33.

The ever increasing trend by Japanese manufacturers toward rounded tail lights is continued throughout the Skyline range

NISSAN SKYLINE GT-R
2.6-litre, five-speed manual

ENGINE
Location	Front
Cylinders	Six-in-line
Bore × stroke	86.0 × 73.7 mm
Capacity	2568cm³
Induction	Electronic fuel injection
Compression ratio	8.5 to 1
Fuel pump	Electric
Valve gear	Cog-belt driven twin ohc four-valves/cyl
Claimed power	211 kW at 6800 rpm
Claimed torque	353 Nm at 4400 rpm
Maximum recommended engine speed	8000 rpm
Specific power output	82.2 kW/litre

TRANSMISSION
Type	Five-speed manual
Driving wheels	Electronically controlled torque split, four-wheel drive
Clutch	Multi, wet plate
Gearbox	

Gear ratio		kmh 1000 rpm	Max Speed	At (rpm)
First	3.214	8.87	71	8000
Second	1.925	14.81	118	8000
Third	1.302	21.89	175	8000
Fourth	1.000	28.51	228	8000
Fifth	0.752	37.91	235	6200
Final-Drive Ratio				4.11 to 1

SUSPENSION
Front	Independent by "multi-link" system - unequal upper and lower control arms with coil springs and anti-roll bar
Rear	Independent by multi-link system with coil springs and anti-roll bar
Wheels	Alloy, 8.0JJ × 16
Tyres	225/50 R16 92V Bridgestone Potenza RE71

BRAKES
Front	ventilated 296 mm discs
Rear	297 mm discs

STEERING
Type	Power assisted rack and pinion, rear steering by shaft/computer controlled gearbox

DIMENSIONS
Wheelbase	2615 mm
Front track	1480 mm
Rear track	1480 mm
Overall length	4545 mm
Overall width	1755 mm
Overall height	1340 mm
Ground clearance	135 mm
Kerb weight	1430 kg
Weight to power	6.8 kg/kW
Fuel tank	72.0 litres

CHECKLIST
Alloy wheels	yes
Adjustable steering	yes
Air-conditioning	yes
Carpets	yes
Central door locking	yes
Clock	yes
Cruise control	no
Intermittent wipers	yes
Laminated screen	yes
Petrol-filler lock	yes
Power steering	yes
Power windows	yes
Radio	yes
Tape player	yes
Compact disc player	no
Rear window wiper	yes
Remote outside mirror adjustment	yes
Sun roof	no
Tachometer	yes
Trip computer	no

ACCELERATION
0-100 km/h	5.05 seconds
Standing 400m	13.47 seconds

Sports seats and leather steering wheel continue the sporty theme in the four door GTS-t.

and when viewed from the rear the GT-R conjures up memories of the early Mazda RX-series rotaries that boasted the round light treatment.

Considering the purpose of the GT-R, its interior appointments are extremely high in specification. Unlike other cars intended to perform race-track duties there are no obvious weight saving measures incorporated into the GT-R's interior. The instrument layout provides a stimulating and functional driving environment.

A large speedometer and tachometer (redlined at 8000 rpm) dominate the dash while an array of secondary switch controls are mounted high around the binnacle within easy finger-tip reach of the steering wheel. Other controls, including a turbo boost gauge, are positioned on a centre console which slopes downwards and integrates with the transmission tunnel. The seats and their lowly-placed position as well as the thick leather gripped three-spoked steering wheel further enhance the interior's sporty theme.

As one may expect of such a car the new GT-R is the toast of the Japanese automotive fraternity. But it doesn't end there. Nissan has big plans for the entire Skyline range — prime target being Toyota's big-selling Cressida.

Unfortunately it has not been decided whether Australia will even get the car at this stage. Insiders say the car is being evaluated and with Nissan's current Australian manufacturing plants being re-tooled to produce the forthcoming AD50 Matilda project, to be shared by Ford and Nissan, the bet is that with such an expansive model line-up the Australian subsidiary will think long and hard before it makes any firm decision.

Word is that Nissan at this stage intends to market the desirable GT-R on the domestic Japanese market only. It seems the Japanese have finally discovered that if you have a car as good as the GT-R you keep it to yourself and it's certain Nissan will have no trouble in finding customers for the compulsory 500 evolution models required under Group A regulations.

From the leather-gripped steering wheel through to the high rear-deck spoiler the Skyline's intentions are clear: to succeed both in the market place and on the world's motor racing circuits. If it does prove successful it will be stamped revolutionary. If it fails you can be sure the number crunchers at Nissan will pour millions of dollars into improving it.

While we don't fully agree with Nissan's claims that the new Skyline has unlimited potential, it certainly elevates the already keen awareness of Japan's unrelenting push towards automotive supremacy. ❏

SKYLINE EVOLUTION

ALS1 (1957).

S54 (1965).

C10 (1970).

C110 (1972).

C210 (1977).

R30 (1981).

R31 (1987).

ET-S 4wd system transfers to front wheels torque that rear wheels can't cope with. Combined with Super-HICAS 4ws, it gives fool-proof handling

It looks like a Tokyo taxi-cab, but underneath it's

THE WORLD'S MOST ADVANCED ROAD CAR

Gavin Green drives the Nissan Skyline GT-R at the Nurburgring

THE PORSCHE 928GT, FIRE-engine red and driven by a professional German racer, could not stand the pace. At the end of another lap of the Nürburgring's 13.02-mile Nordschleife circuit, with the Nissan Skyline poised to overtake, smoke started to billow from the rear of the German car. The incapacitated Porsche, smoking impotently, silently pulled off the circuit. The Nissan hurtled on its way.

On the Nürburgring's long back straight, just before the blow-up, the Porsche had actually pulled a couple of car lengths on the Nissan. A 928GT, after all, has more power than a standard Skyline GT-R. It's more aerodynamic, too. But on the winding mountainous part of the circuit – which, to be frank, is the rest of the Nürburgring – the Japanese car was convincingly its superior.

The Skyline neatly and quite effortlessly strung together the brows, dips and apices that constitute this most dangerous and challenging of racing circuits. The Porsche, indomitable by conventional front-engined supercar standards, was leaning and scrubbing, sliding and screeching. It was being out-manoeuvred. Not by a

conventional supercar, mind you. The Porsche was being licked by the world's most advanced road car.

With the Skyline, Nissan's engineers were given a free hand – in the words of one of them – 'to out-Porsche Porsche. We reckon Porsche makes the best-handling cars. And the 959 is reckoned to be the most advanced supercar ever made. We wanted to beat the 959.'

Nissan also built the GT-R to win international group A races, against the likes of the Cosworth Sierra and the BMW M3. A minimum of 5000 will be built although, such is the demand in Japan, the volume is likely to be considerably bigger. There are no plans yet for European sales.

The starting point for the GT-R is fairly humble: a standard three-door version of the Skyline, Nissan's Toyota Cressida rival. Add big butch

metal wheel-arch flares, ellipsoidal headlamps (with lenses like a projector's), and meaty 225/50R16 Bridgestone Potenza tyres riding on starfish-pattern alloys. To reduce weight, the bonnet and front wings are aluminium. Fully kitted, the GT-R looks fairly discreet, especially in the gunmetal grey of our test car (the most common colour).

To give this new road-racer some bite, Nissan's long-serving big straight-six gets twin-cam, four valves per cylinder heads and, more important, a pair of ceramic turbos. Maximum power, for the 2.6-litre unit, is claimed to be 280bhp but one of the Nissan engineers on hand at the Nürburgring explained that Japanese manufacturers have a gentlemen's agreement not to build cars with more than 280bhp: 'In fact,' he whispered, 'the GT-R has an easy 300bhp,

and we can tweak it to give more.' The ceramic turbos are a novel touch; they have far better heat resistance than conventional steel turbo rotors.

Far more important than what's in the nose is what is under the floorpan. The drivetrain – dubbed Nissan's Electronic Torque Split 4wd system (E-TS for short) – is a rear-drive-biased set-up that can deliver anything between zero and 50 percent of the torque to the front wheels. In simple terms, the front wheels get the driving torque that the rear wheels can't handle. When the GT-R starts to oversteer, or breaks traction in some other way at the tail, power is fed to the front.

The 'brain' of the system is a microprocessor that gathers signals from sensors monitoring lateral g, throttle opening and engine speed. This chip, in turn, is linked to another chip – also used to control the ABS – which measures wheel speed and longitudinal g. The main microprocessor gathers all the relevant information and, in turn, actuates a hydraulic pressure control valve which varies the engagement pressure on a wet multi-plate clutch – the main mechanical component in the 4wd system.

This clutch, in the heart of the transfer unit, feeds torque to the front wheels. By varying the level of hydraulic pressure applied to the clutch, the front/rear torque split can be continuously controlled from rear-drive only (0:100) to a rigid 4wd mode (50:50), or any split in between.

When the multi-plate clutch is engaged, drive is fed to the front wheels via a chain linked to a forward-facing driveshaft, and the front differential. Drive is fed to the rear wheels via the main shaft of the transfer unit, just as in a conventional rear-drive car.

The endless variability of the front-to-rear torque split is one of the keys of the system: most performance 4wd vehicles, which usually feature viscous coupling control, have some degree of variability, but nothing like the range of the GT-R's system. Nissan reckons its electro-mechanical system is superior to that of a viscous coupling controlled centre diff: the VC is sensitive to rotation, whereas the E-TS system is torque-sensitive.

The Porsche 959 also has an electro-mechanical set-up, but it always has a minimum 20 percent of the torque fed to the front wheels. The fact that some of the torque goes forwards compromises the 959's ultimate handling: any car with some torque being fed through the front wheels is more likely to understeer than a properly set-up rear-drive car. The Nissan behaves like a rear-drive car, until the eventual want of rear traction summons the front wheels into action.

The high-tech theme of the GT-R doesn't end with the transmission, though. Four-wheel steering helps turn-in, and improves the stability of the car while cornering. Unlike the cruder systems used by Mazda and Honda, the GT-R's four-wheel steering is used to improve handling, rather than parking ease.

'With the Skyline, Nissan's engineers were given a free hand - in their words - "to out-Porsche Porsche"'

The rear wheels counter-steer to help the Skyline turn into the corner, and then steer in the same direction as the fronts, to help stability. The rear wheels on the 4ws Honda Prelude, by comparison, counter-steer only in very tight corners and during parking; on the 4ws Mazda 626 the rears counter-steer only when parking.

Sensors monitor the steering angle, the speed with which the steering wheel is being manoeuvred, and the vehicle's velocity. The information is fed to a microchip which controls a solenoid valve which, in turn, controls the oil flow to a rear hydraulic actuator. The rear actuator steers the rear wheels via a pair of track rods. Unlike the original Nissan HICAS 4ws system, there is no compliance in the GT-R's set-up. The track rods can articulate the rear wheels to a maximum of one degree. At high speed, though, the maximum movement – in both directions – is approximately 0.3deg.

A final avant-garde touch is the use of Nissan's new all-round multi-link suspension – also seen on the new 300ZX, and to be a feature of the next-generation Bluebird (to be called Primera). The front suspension – the more intriguing – is based on the double-wishbone principle, but uses a third link at the outer end of the upper wishbone. This articulates the upper arm's behaviour, improving ride and camber control – and thus steering feel. Another advantage: the multi-link set-up

'It soon became clear: the GT-R driven by journalists was faster than the German supercars driven by pros'

is supposed to improve damper control: every inch the wheel moves, the damper moves by exactly the same amount. Anti-roll bars are fitted front and rear and, compared with the normal Skyline, the springs and dampers are noticeably stiffer.

On paper, then, we have a technological wonder car. Out there, we had the Nürburgring, the world's most testing circuit. We joined a small group of Japanese journalists, flown to Germany to try Nissan's new supercar on the toughest course imaginable. Quite by chance, the German magazine Auto Bild also hired the Nordschleife part of the 'Ring – in effect, the old Nürburgring, minus the newly fettled grand prix track – and a few professional racers to help with a comparison it was doing between a 928GT, a Mercedes 500SL and the new BMW M5. It soon became clear: in terms of lap times, the GT-R driven by journalists was faster than the German trio driven by professionals. It was an unexpected bonus for Nissan.

Inside, the Skyline is new-school Japanese. All the gargoyles and gimmickry of old Japanese performance cars are gone. Instead, you're left with a sombre, subdued cabin: dark colours, a nicely sculpted dash, and a full house of analogue instruments – including one I've never seen before: a torque-split gauge, which shows exactly how much muscle is being sent to the front diff.

The seats are big, and hug

the thighs and torso. The driving position is straight-ahead, and perfect: the pedals are placed by people who know what drivers like. The steering wheel, three-spoked and leather-rimmed, looks beautiful and feels good. The gear lever, leather-crowned, selects first a little notchily, but flows through the other ratios. Only the switchgear – hard plastic, and rather cheap – spoils the upmarket effect.

It was time to try the 'Ring. The clutch is firm, the engine pulls comfortably from low revs, growing increasingly truculent as the revs build. The deep engine note turns into a growl, and then into a bellow. The turbos come in quite smoothly, but when they're engaged, the GT-R surges forward: even in a straight line, it feels like a pukka supercar. To boot, the big six is smooth, refined.

Turn right out of the Nordschleife's pits, onto the circuit proper, and soon you're through a left-hander and surging downhill – with the new grand-prix track clearly in view off to the left – heading to the tightest complex on the circuit. It doesn't take long to realise that this Skyline is different: it turns into corners with an extra, artificial eagerness: it's quite pronounced.

On these tighter corners, the car is a basic understeerer: but there's less nose plough than on an Audi Quattro, or even a Porsche 959. The rear counter-steer helps overcome initial understeer. So does the fact that, on tight corners in the dry, no power whatsoever is being fed to the front tyres: driven wheels tend to have larger cornering slip angles. Nissan's engineers reckon that in fast driving on a dry road, no more than 20 percent of the available torque is fed to the front.

Through the tight bits, on the first kilometre of the circuit, body

roll is well checked, and the car neatly strings together the corners. Soon after, the circuit opens up: blind crests lead to fast corners. The circuit dips and curls, winding its way between pine forests, lined with Armco, but with worryingly small run-off areas. Leave the track, and you'll almost certainly end up kissing the barriers – hard.

On the faster corners, the car's behaviour is also foreign. The car obediently turns into the bend – helped by the tail counter-steer – before drifting neutrally through the turn. Stability is helped by the rear wheels which, when cornering, turn in the same direction as the fronts. Keep the right boot down, and you'll probably just start to feel the onset of oversteer – the tail is just starting to swing wide of the nose – and everything you've been taught tells you to back off and wind on some opposite lock, to check the rear-end slide. But in a GT-R you keep your foot hard down, and don't have to worry about any steering correction.

Just as the tail starts to move, it is denied some of the power – which instead is fed to the front. The rear tyre slip angle is thus reduced, and the front

'The GT-R flatters your driving, giving traction and security where a normal car would bite'

increased. And by keeping the car on full throttle – and thus losing no time – the car magically straightens its line, and exits the corner tidily and neatly, with no tail-out nonsense. No need to correct the steering, or to back off. No need to do anything except steer the car normally. The car does the correcting for you.

No car, of course, can totally overcome bozo driving: plough into a corner way too fast, and you'll still end up arguing with the crash barrier. Instead, the GT-R flatters your driving, making ham-fisted drivers smoother, and giving extra traction and security where a normal car would bite.

It's well-suited to the Nürburgring: to the twists and brows and turns, for the handling is the most impressive aspect of the car. Just as important, no driver can learn the Nürburgring in the

short time (barely a day) that we had available. As a result, we were all making small mistakes, as we misread corners. The Skyline compensated for our misjudgments.

The most memorable lap was when I followed the bright red Porsche, which was being driven hard by a man who knew the circuit better than I. The 928GT, of course, is among the finest of all rear-drive cars: stable, poised, and fast. Yet, slowly but surely, the GT-R narrowed the gap. Whereas the tail of the Porsche would sway quite alarmingly at times, the GT-R would be smoother, more composed. The GT-R was quicker around the bends – particularly the slower and medium-speed turns.

I reckon I pulled in about 10 car lengths on the 928, in the course of a lap. Sweeping down to the chicane that slows the cars before completing a lap,

the 928 had had enough: smoke billowed ominously. An hour later, the Porsche was going again, so the problem cannot have been catastrophic. Yet the Skyline had beaten the German car, fair and square.

For the 13.02 miles, my best lap – timed rather haphazardly on a conventional wrist watch – was a few seconds under nine minutes. Nissan's fastest test driver, who tests frequently at the Nordschleife, has nipped below 8min 30sec. That's an *average* speed of more than 90mph. It's the same average speed that Fangio managed, when setting fastest lap on his way to winning the '57 German Grand Prix, in a Maserati 250F. That, incidentally, was one of the Great Man's greatest drives.

But whereas Fangio's lap must have been full of lurid oversteer slides, and must have summoned every last ounce of talent from the world's greatest-ever racer, the Japanese gentleman who matched his speed in a standard Nissan road car probably barely raised a sweat. The car's talent helped make him a Fangio. Although not the most inspiring, accelerative, or beautiful of cars, the Skyline is now surely the world's most awesomely competent road machine.

Counterpoint

A WEEK BEFORE FLYING TO
Germany to drive the new
Nissan at the Nürburgring, I
took delivery of my own GT-R.
For two years I'd been hearing
stories about the forthcoming
new super Skyline. Nissan
engineers were unanimous:
this was the greatest road car
ever to come from Japan. The
new 300ZX, developed
concurrently, and subsequently
lauded by the world's press,
generated far less enthusiasm.
The enthusiasm became
infectious. Even before driving a
GT-R, I ordered one. In Japan, it
costs just under £20,000 –
which makes it about 40 percent
more expensive than a Toyota
Supra Turbo or a fully loaded
Celica GT-4.

The moment I knew that I had
chosen something special came
on a race track, when I first
drove the car in Japan. After a
learning lap, I picked up the
pace and entered a tight left-
hander a bit too fast, bringing
the tail around. In itself, the car's
behaviour was benign, with
good feedback from the front
tyres and plenty of evidence of
the developing yaw.

My first reaction was to ease

'I dived into my first lap with a confidence that a previous drive in a less powerful car had not allowed'

off the accelerator. That's what
I had been taught: a rear-end
slide is caused by wheelspin, so
contain the wheelspin to control
the slide. But in studying the
literature explaining the new
E-TS (Electronic Torque Split)
four-wheel-drive system I had
noticed that wheelspin would be
reduced by the system's own
devices, and that the result
would be better cornering
behaviour. Having already
determined that there was
sufficient space to contain a
spin, I slammed the accelerator
pedal to the floor.

The sudden surge of power
increased the amount of
wheelspin at the rear, causing
the car to yaw, but as the rear
wheels spun, the E-TS
computer tightened up the
multi-plate transfer clutch
connecting drive to the front
wheels, so that a gradually
increasing proportion of the
engine's torque was deducted

from that going to the rear
wheels and went to the front
wheels instead.

The ET-S reduced the
wheelspin that was causing the
rear to slide, and put the car on
course for recovery.

The system can also be used
to tame understeer. The natural
chassis balance is towards
understeer, but if it builds up,
the driver can counteract it with
a boot-full of power to start the
rear sliding. That will work in
almost any high-powered rear-
drive car, but in most of them
the driver is then faced with
catching a rapid increase in
yaw. In the Skyline GT-R,
however, the actions that follow
are the same as if the car had
started in a slide, and the end
result is just as benign.

This revolutionary ability to
use the variable torque split to
control the car's attitude makes
the Skyline a virtually foolproof
handler. Aided by fine basic

suspension geometry, and the
clever ministrations of Super-
HICAS four-wheel steering, the
GT-R is an easy car to drive
hard and fast, and I was able
to dive into my first lap at the
Nürburgring with an enthusiasm
and confidence that a previous
drive in a less powerful rear-
drive car had not allowed.

By comparison, Gavin Green
drove the car with more delicacy
and precision, to keep the car
cornering as a racing car
should. Driven in that manner
it is as quick as any current
production car, bar a Ferrari F40.

But it seems to me that he was
not using the car's full ability.
He has years of racing
experience which have taught
him to anticipate certain limits
that, I believe, the Skyline
transcends. For him, the Skyline
probably requires an unlearning
period, and in the hands of
Nissan test drivers who have
unlearned already, the Skyline is
demonstrably superior to rivals.

But the point about it for me
is not what its final ability might
be. More important for the
average enthusiast, is the
ability to go quickly and have
fun straight away. And I don't
know of any car that achieves
that aim better than the GT-R.
That's why I just had to have
one. **Kevin Radley**

The Nissan that leaves the Sierra Cosworth standing

Nissan's four-wheel-drive, four-wheel-steer Skyline GT-R is not readily available in Europe, but Jeremy Walton has driven the powerful homologation special on UK roads

STAN PAPIOR

NAME A TECHNICAL FEATURE AND the Nissan Skyline GT-R seemingly has it crammed under its bulbous body somewhere. Electronically-managed four-wheel drive, four-wheel steering, twin overhead camshafts and 24 valves, a double ration of turbochargers — it's all there. But the Skyline's secret is that it puts all that technology to such good use in everyday motoring.

Most homologation specials are built only to meet international motorsport regulations and can be a bit rough around the edges in road-going form. The BMW M3, Ford Sierra RS Cosworth and Lancia Delta Integrale have some obvious deficiencies for use in the UK — the Lancia and BMW are left-hand-drive only, while the Sierra is equipped with an engine that is coarse and unrefined. They all have great chassis, to be sure, but the complete motoring packages are flawed.

None of these flaws mars the right-hand-drive Nissan. In fact, the Skyline was described by a Rolls-Royce owner as having "a smoother engine than my car and excellent road manners".

More than 12,000 GT-Rs have been sold in Japan since September last year, at a current price of Y4.45 million (£17,800), but Nissan has consistently blocked its sale in Europe as a road car, already embarrassed by continued demand in Japan beyond the planned production run of 5000 units.

Up to 50 per cent of available torque is fed to front wheels when rear wheels start to lose grip. Roadholding and balance are superb. Janspeed chip boosts power

Chunky Skyline GT-R looks the part; bonnet and wings are alloy, body kit and deformable front panels are plastic. Strong demand in Japan has so far prevented sale of car in Europe. Skyline's welter of technology is put to good use; GT-R is a fine all-rounder

◀ However, we had a unique opportunity to drive one on British roads. The personal import belongs to John Kirkham, a Midlander who owns several such Cosworth-crushing devices.

The Skyline should easily be capable of achieving Nissan's modest performance claims, its 2.6-litre straight six officially churning out 280bhp (the unofficial Japanese maximum horsepower quotation) at 6800rpm and 260lb ft of torque at 4400rpm. Based on independent figures obtained by *Car Graphic* magazine in Japan, there is good reason to believe the GT-R actually has more than 300bhp. The car recorded a 0-62mph time of 5.6secs, 0-100mph in 13.3secs and a standing quarter-mile time of 13.8secs at 100.6mph. Those figures trample all over the Sierra Cosworth's efforts.

Nissan says the top speed is "over 250km/h" (155mph), although the *Car Graphic* example was limited to 112mph in fourth and fifth.

The dark blue Kirkham car certainly looks the part, with aggressive, bulbous lines and distinctive ellipsoidal headlamps. The body kit and deformable front panels are made of plastic, while the wings and bonnet are alloy.

Although the wings weigh just 2.2lb each, the Skyline tips the scales at a hefty 3217lb. However, the powerful engine, chassis dynamics and brakes are all up to the task.

Under the acronym ATTESA E-TS (Advanced Total Traction Engineering System for All terrains and Electronic Torque Split), Nissan has adapted the conventional Skyline's rear-wheel-drive layout to cope with the demands of 280bhp by supplying up to 50 per cent of available torque to the front wheels.

A microprocessor controls a central multi-plate clutch that is activated by hydraulic pressure. Sensors — some of which are shared with the anti-lock braking system — send information such as throttle opening, lateral

and longitudinal g forces and comparative front and rear wheel speeds to the micro-processor, and when the rear wheels start to lose grip, the pressurised clutch plates pass power to the front wheels via a Morse chain and shaft.

A 'Front Kg-m Torque' meter tells the driver how much of the rear-drive effort is being apportioned forward (up to 50 per cent). Under hard acceleration, about 15 to 20 per cent is routinely diverted to the front, while the harshest cornering seems to allow a 25/75 split. However, the power split is 50/50 when the car pulls away with the front wheels on tarmac and the rear wheels on dirt, for example.

Rear-wheel drive, which is the normal state of the GT-R in unstressed circumstances, is achieved by a conventional propeller shaft to an independent rear end — one that shares its sophisticated multi-link set-up and most components with the rear-drive 300ZX.

The Skyline also enlists the help of Nissan's Super HICAS four-wheel steering system. Four sensors gather information on steering column shaft angles (and the speed of driver inputs), as well as road speed, lateral g forces and engine revs. Acting on these factors, a solenoid-controlled valve releases high-pressure hydraulic fluid to activate the rear track rod system.

The rear wheels first counter-steer (to a maximum of 1.5deg) then turn in the same direction as the front wheels to hasten the car into the turn then provide maximum stability.

Steering is by power-assisted rack and pinion, offering a fine blend of sharp, sensitive response at speed and effortless parking.

The clutch engages smoothly and man-oeuvring in tight spaces is only complicated by the softly rounded body contours and high rear spoiler, both of which can make it initially difficult to place the car accurately. After 20 miles or so, it becomes second nature. Then the

NISSAN SKYLINE GT-R

LAYOUT
Longitudinal front engine/four-wheel drive
ENGINE
Capacity 2568cc, 6 cylinders in line
Bore 86mm, **stroke** 73.7mm
Compression ratio 8.5 to 1
Head/block alloy/cast iron
Valve gear dohc, 4 valves per cylinder
Fuel and ignition Electronic fuel injection with digital electronic injection and electronic management. Twin Garrett AiResearch T25 turbochargers, ceramic rotors, intercooler
Max power (claimed) 280bhp (PS-Din) (209kW ISO) at 6800rpm
Max torque 260lb ft (353 Nm) at 4400rpm
GEARBOX
Five-speed manual
Ratios top 0.752, 4th 1.00, 3rd 1.302, 2nd 1.925, 1st 3.214
Final drive ratio 4.111, limited slip by multiple plates 23.29mph/1000rpm in top
SUSPENSION
Front, offset geometry, double wishbones, alloy tubs and uprights, anti-roll bar, coil springs and dampers
Rear, independent, multi-link, double wishbones, coil springs and dampers
STEERING
Power assisted, Super HICAS four-wheel steer
WHEELS AND TYRES
Forged aluminium alloy, 8ins rims. 225/50 Bridgestone RE71 tyres
PERFORMANCE (claimed)
0-62mph (100km/h) 5.6secs
0-100mph (161km/h) 13.3secs
Standing quarter mile 13.8secs
Maximum speed 155mph
FUEL CONSUMPTION (claimed)
18.9mpg
PRICE
Total (in UK) £35,000 (estimated, for personal import)

Interior is uninspiring in dour grey, but is well equipped and neatly laid out. Driver is confronted by a comprehensive range of gauges

Twin-turbo 2.6-litre six is smooth, flexible and free-revving; performance is stunning with 'official' output of 280bhp. GT-R reaches 62mph in 5.6secs

Skyline feels its modest 15ft length and 5ft 9ins breadth.

However, you never lose the feeling that the enormous ventilated disc brakes — clamped by racing-style four-piston calipers at the front — are working hard. They must cope with a kerb weight in excess of 330lb beyond that of the substantial Cosworth 4x4, as well as significantly more power.

Beneath a welter of emotive marketing labels, the twin-turbo 2.6-litre straight six chuffs sibilantly at a steady 700rpm or transcends 7000rpm with muted vigour. It is very refined and smooth, even in the 7400 to 8000rpm warning zone of the 10,000rpm tachometer.

If the free-spinning engine is a major attraction, then the five-speed gearbox is a minor distraction. The first four ratios work with the usual Japanese slick efficiency, but the fourth-fifth shift is distinctly awkward. The gear lever almost fouls the handbrake in the manner of TVRs.

The gear ratios, though, are a revelation; the Nissan proves very flexible and accelerates with the assured deftness of a poker player who has hit a golden streak. At 8000rpm in the first two slots, the equivalent of 43 and 71mph is reported. Third gear stretches to more than 100mph, while fourth thrusts the GT-R to an indicated 130mph, at 6700rpm.

Fifth is called on only for its cruising virtues, but these are interrupted at 121mph by repellent chimes. At 120mph and 5150rpm, the Nissan settles surely into an all-day pace — one that is more relaxing than any sports special and compares for subdued progress alongside a BMW 535i.

At the lower end of the speed range, the turbochargers provide discernible boost from 2000rpm (47mph) in fifth. Just 700rpm later, half the available boost (12.8psi) prods the

bespoiled Skyline from 63mph towards the 4400rpm torque peak, just beyond 100mph.

Until deliberately provoked, there is never any indication that the car has reached its enormous — almost unnerving — limits. The 225/50 Bridgestone RE71 tyres are more than a match for the car's cornering ability.

The basic handling characteristic is stable understeer, which is simply amplified if the driver gets too enthusiastic. An oversteer power slide is virtually out of the question.

The nimble handling is matched by a ride quality that is supple and well controlled in its reactions to bumps and ripples, although at low speeds the ride becomes slightly jiggly.

Inside, the GT-R does not earn points for eye appeal, but the seats, covered in dour grey fabric, are comfortable and very supportive. The driver is confronted by a daunting bank of 10 dials, but they are all legible and the oversized speedometer and Tomei-brand rev-counter are perfectly placed.

After driving the standard GT-R, we tried it with a Janspeed microprocessor chip that boosted power by an extra 70bhp. Hand timing indicated a 0-62mph time of just 4.9secs. The Kirkham GT-R became positively animated, writhing away from standing starts with the 370bhp alacrity that Janspeed heir Kieth Odor enjoyed when winning the 1990 production class at Spa Francorchamps.

The GT-R may not have the charisma of an Integrale or an M3, but it is one of the most comfortably capable and civilised performance cars you are likely to experience. Amid the plethora of Nissan acronyms, I am convinced that the 'R' in GT-R stands for Respect. A corporate leopard really can change its spots. Cars like the GT-R, 300ZX, 200SX and Primera show an imposing breadth of engineering ability. If only it would allow European sales of its best technology advertisement — the Skyline GT-R. ■

GOD ZILLA!

Finally unleashed at mid-season, the Skyline GT-R supercar from Nissan trampled the field in the Australian Touring Car Championship's last round, where Jim Richards clinched his third championship. But about that nickname. Competition Editor Jonathan Ingram reports. Photography by Race Press Australia.

IT TERRORIZED THE AUSTRALIAN TOURING CAR neighborhood even before it arrived, with ▉competition▉ word of its impending arrival on the shores of the South Continent circulating anxiously. When it finally landed, the vehicle sent competitors fleeing in all directions for the proper adjectives to invoke the wrath of the rule makers, an unseemly demonstration in a country known for its manliness. Finally, when it rolled onto the tarmac for the first time at a race meeting, fear met imagination with a combustive swirl in the mind of a mechanic, who remarked cooly, "There it sits -- Godzilla."

Like crowds trampling one another to flee the oncoming menace, they've been running from Godzilla ever since. Not just the competition, but the folks at Nissan Australia, as well. Like Dr. Frankenstein running from his own shoes-of-lead monster, the folks at Nissan have been running from this gawd-awful nickname of

Godzilla, which follows them with arms outstretched wherever they go on the island continent. Meanwhile, the news of Godzilla is circulated worldwide by humble journalists, merely looking for a nice handle.

So this is truly an extraordinary racing car -- one that scares its own factory and team representatives as well as the competition. It could not have been a more distasteful nickname for Nissan's otherwise elegance-on-steroids design. It's an aerodynamically smooth, race-homologated iteration of the roadgoing Skyline (SCI, September 1990). Powerful, too, with all-wheel drive and steering, twin turbos, scads of horsepower and oomph. There are no strands of plastic drool hanging from any air-sucking oval grill full of chrome teeth, nor is there any evidence the car eats small children and household pets for lunch.

In appearance, the GT-R stands between the old fold-and-crease school of Japanese design and the swoopy swirls of the most recent generation. In truth, the first Group A car from Holden built by Tom Walkinshaw Racing in a wind tunnel in England looked more like something out of a B-grade Japanese monster flick -- or something David Lynch dreamed up between *Eraserhead* and *Blue Velvet*. No, it's the ordnance underneath the Skyline's body that makes the competitors, who drive Ford Sierras and Holden Commodore VLs, feel like they may be facing a nuclear warhead with popguns.

The GT-R reflects Nissan's effort to take its engineering pursuits worldwide. The inline six engine is force inducted by twin turbos and a fuel delivery system designed by the lads on the US Left Coast who work at Nissan Performance Technology, Inc., the racing subsidiary of Nissan's American offices. It's the same crowd which has had the IMSA GTP category by the tail for the last three years and which has electronics whizbanger Don Devendorf computing all the black-box magic. In the Skyline GT-R, the electronic delivery system provided a 70-horsepower jump in power over the Japanese version for the 2.6 liter engine, which in race trim now generates 700 bhp at 6,000 rpm.

touring car

The Skyline GT-R is, in fact, treated somewhat like a movie star by Nissan. In Japan, the company reportedly received 5,000 orders for the 500 homologation specials required for Touring Car status. The car is also treated like a star by Nissan Motorsport Australia, the racing team owned and operated by Fred Gibson, whose small factory is located across the road from the company headquarters in Dandenong, outside of Melbourne. Specifically, journalists are not permitted up-close audiences with the vehicle, if that can be avoided. In the wake of their proven ability to spread the car's hated nickname, journalists are shown none of the equipment pertinent to the car's performance lest some details of the car's enormous potential be leaked, enabling competitors and rule makers to rail against it. A nickname of Godzilla, after all, is bad enough.

Being an outlander, your American journalist arrived at the headquarters building for an escort to the race shop, unaware of these machinations. Sorry, this Ameri-

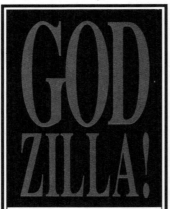

GOD ZILLA!

"In truth, the first Group A car from Holden built by Tom Walkinshaw Racing in a wind tunnel in England looked more like something out of a B-grade Japanese monster flick -- or something David Lynch dreamed up between Eraserhead and Blue Velvet."

Above: Gentleman Jim Richards
. . . .

can was told, it's too early in the day. You'll have to come back. By the time I returned later in the day and was driven to the race car shop, surprise! Both Godzillas had been stabled in the transport truck for the trip to Adelaide's special one-off street races for Touring Cars.

The good news: Jim Richards, who won the Touring Car Championship by piloting the GT-R to victory in the final race of the season at Oran Park, was ready for questions. So was Mark Skaife, test driver for the GT-R as well as pilot of the team's second Skyline in the Touring Car Championship. Your reporter was ready, too. "Where did this name Godzilla come from?" I asked cheerfully.

Oh, well, all the questions can't be winners. Quickly the conversation moved on to how Richards won the Touring Car championship in the final round at Oran Park, where four drivers entered the season's final event with the possibility of winning the championship. That group included folk heroes Dick Johnson and Peter Brock, both chauffeuring Sierras. Richards drove the new GT-R, despite the fact it had only been raced from mid-season on, experiencing brake and suspension reliability problems in initial outings.

finale

In the season finale, however, Richards won the pole and the race,

and thus clinched his third career Australian Touring Car Championship. It was a classy conclusion to the most competitive season in 31 years Down Under for the ever-popular Touring Car category, where Richards' hairline may be receding but his reputation is still oncoming. He is considered perhaps the best Touring Car driver in Australia, although he does not have the larger-than-life standing of Johnson or Brock. Richards began his career in go-karts in native New Zealand, where his father was a mechanic. Racing, he said, "seemed better than standing in line at the dole queue."

Oddly enough, he too has a despised nickname – Gentleman Jim. Dauntless in the face of adversity, this reporter asked him how he got tagged with that handle. "Oh," he said with a mischievous grin, "whenever I look in the rearview mirror and see that someone is faster than me, I just pull over and let him pass." It was, in fact, a humorous and gentlemanly answer from an easygoing man who is often hell on wheels. After the laughter subsides, he adds, "I've been involved in a few skirmishes in my time."

The reputation of the GT-R is oncoming, too, as it gradually matches its pre-appearance build-up as a supercar. Richards maintains that 640 bhp is a "good talking point" for the car's power, even though other estimates have it closer to 700. As it is, the rule makers have given the Skyline 160 additional kilos of weight (353 lbs.) compared to the Sierras. The Nissan remains faster in a straight line, still, at the outset of the development curve. The trick, then, is stopping it and its additional weight.

weak brakes

The car was homologated with water-cooled brakes, but the front discs are only 14.8 inches and the rears 13 inches with six-pot calipers. Never, says Richards, have drivers returned to the pits with praise for the brakes. In longer races, the car must stop more often for brake pad changes. Early problems with suspension and drivetrain pieces breaking under pressure from Ford Sierras were resolved by locally sourcing the driveshafts, CV joints, and wheel hubs.

The Nissan's advantage (other than horsepower) is better tire wear due to all-wheel drive, which enables the team to use softer compound tires than on the preceding GT-S rear-wheel drive version of the Skyline. "The hardest thing about the all-wheel drive is you can't throw the car around," says Richards. "When it gets out of shape, you have to wait until it slows enough to the speed where all wheels will get traction."

The system has front-wheel drive connected by a front-mounted multi-plate clutch. Drive torque is distributed variably to the front and rear axles. The rear differential is also controlled continuously. It is very much like the drive system Porsche developed for the 959 and its race car derivative, the 961.

Depending on pre-selected programs, the four-wheel-drive controller calculates corresponding torque-split values for the center and rear differentials from engine output, wheel speeds, and other vehicle parameters such as axle loads. These values are then set by the hydraulic system, which modulates the variable all-wheel drive.

The trick in a race car is selecting the right computer chip for the black box to run the all-wheel drive system, which depends on the nature of the course. The next trick becomes setting up the car's suspension to derive the most advantage from all-wheel drive, where in race trim most of the power is devoted to the rear wheels. The Nissan Motorsport Australia team eventually discovered that setting up the car as if it was rear-wheel drive first, then dialing in the all-wheel system cut down on variables worked best. So far, the team has simply eliminated all-wheel steer from its program.

mount panorama

The crowning glory of Australian auto racing is the Mount Panorama event near Bathurst (SCI, March 1990). That is the supreme test of durability over 1,000 kilometers of uphill and downhill high-speed racing. Because of its longer distance, however, it is not included in the Touring Car championship, where events run less than one hour. When Nissan Motorsports Australia arrived at Bathurst with its new GT-R shortly after clinching the championship, the competition was certain of its superiority. Until Richards immediately took

the lead from eleventh on the grid, where the team started after qualifying on Yokohama race rubber.

"We went from eleventh to first in seven laps," said Richards. "We knew what their cars could do. The opposition didn't know what ours could do, though. They couldn't believe it. They had their heads in the bloody sand." Eventually, the Nissan effort on the mountain was slowed by a broken spark plug electrode that proved difficult to find. The team made a valiant effort to finish after repairs and ended up with the fastest race lap -- two seconds clear of any other entry,

including the winning Commodore of Allan Grice and Win Percy. Shortly thereafter, Richards added some satisfaction by winning in the streets of Adelaide in a sprint race prior to the Formula One finale, where Skaife unfortunately trashed the newest chassis by putting it on its roof -- to applause from journalists finally able to see the underside.

"I think the opposition has reasonable respect for the car now," says Richards with another understated grin. The Skyline GT-R has indeed lived up to its nickname.

sci

The Correvit couldn't spit the information out fast enough. We knew it was a good run, but we still weren't prepared for the standing 400 metre time. From a launch that smacked your head against the headrest, the Nissan Skyline GT-R offered itself to the breeze, pushing the envelope with every gear change.

Lackety-lackety-lackety ... the printer took a lifetime to punch out the numbers against the background of a twin turbo straight six winding down. Finally, the figures came through: 13.7 seconds; 159.7 km/h. That's *quick*. We laughed with the sheer elation of turning such savage motion into tangible numbers. For a moment, we could grasp what it was like for Jim Richards and Mark Skaife.

From the front, it's all puffed guards, fat paws and squinting eyes; it is, as some would say, one tuff muther. Okay, American muscle cars of the late '60s recorded faster times out of the blocks, but that's *all* they did. That the Skyline is equally challenging and exhilarating across sinuous stretches makes it a very special coupe indeed.

Born of a desire to tear the heart out of all Group A Touring Cars now and yet to come, the white-hot Skyline was always going to be one for the record books. It's a product of '901', the methodology behind Nissan's desire to become the world's Number One car maker in the 1990s. To do that, it acknowledged it had to lift its design and engineering game. It had to build cars like the Skyline GT-R.

The backroom boys took the long handle and included almost every piece of advanced technology at their disposal. And, according to the 901 philosophy, it all had to come together in a manner that made the GT-R satisfying to drive. It wasn't designed to flesh out a flowery brochure, it was designed to *work...*

An appointment with the Calder drag strip followed a routinely slow passage through Melbourne's blocked arterials. The GT-R's flicknife character took a back seat while jostling for space with alarmingly wayward taxis in the economically (and psychologically) depressed CBD.

Mental notes began to stack up. The GT-R doesn't like small amplitude bumps, causing light suspension patter and drumming through the cabin, and potholes confirm via your vertebrae that this is a tightly suspended car. Bucket seats cuddle tighter than a lonely aunt; the steering wheel is thick rimmed and soft to touch, and the clutch, although heavy on first acquaintance, becomes co-operative once leg muscles adapt.

The twin turbo 2.6 litre powerplant was oblivious to our staccato progress. Brushing the throttle was the only requirement for a clean take off on the flat,

BLOOD SPORTS

**An awesome combination of applied science and brute force engineering grabbed Group A by the throat. Now, Nissan has unleashed the beast in road-going form...
Ewen Page drove the Skyline GT-R**

belying the GT-R's tremendous reserves of mechanical angst, reserved for the higher rev ranges.

It was so easy, whether kerb crawling in first gear with no pressure on the throttle pedal, or prematurely selecting the next ratio with the tacho needle nudging 2000 rpm. Rolling on or off the throttle at very low revs wasn't accompanied by the nervous spasms associated with less refined transmissions.

The assisted six has oodles of torque for low engine and road speed running, but 355 Nm of twisting force doesn't

has the most useable fourth gear you'll ever find and, yes, it's cause for a significant increase in blood pressure – but that ain't the whole story. Turning at each extreme via the Super HICAS four-wheel steering system, the GT-R is a handling and roadholding revelation for a car of its weight.

With the first decent deviation, there was no overriding sensation of body roll, or even weight shift. Up to seven-tenths, you could run a spirit level across the bonnet and find the GT-R sitting flat. The overriding impression is of G force; heavy and sustained while ever the steering wheel points away from the horizontal.

And at seven-tenths, the GT-R is so neutral and so bloody fast that it's mentally awkward to push harder. In fact, it's so good most drivers will have to face the challenge of catching up with the car before getting more adventurous. Even driving a BMW M5 doesn't prepare you for the GT-R's demands on concentration and depth perception when shifting hard.

Not that it's a difficult car to punt swiftly. Its limits are so high that you will traverse in comfort any piece of road that at the same pace would leave a Commodore Group A driver wide-eyed – but it will exceed most drivers' accustomed limits long before it wants to go bush. Reading the road ahead and processing information at a rate more rapid than anything you're used to is an art form that takes considerable care to learn. Ham-fisted back street heroes need not apply.

Your instincts tell you that when this thing lets go, it won't be pretty. Not true. Open sweepers can be attacked in a sweet, flowing arc, with the steering and chassis encouraging satellite accuracy. Roll steer is negligable, with the effect of four-wheel steering evident only on turn-in to tightening corners at high speed.

At 3000 revs, there are signs of interest from under the bonnet. Hit four grand, and the world's a beautiful place

arrive until 4400 rpm, when both turbochargers' ceramic impellers are gleefully spinning like tops. It's turbo lag territory below this point, as a relatively naturally aspirated engine attempts to haul 1530 kg while your right boot's stomping against the plate.

At 3000 revs, there are signs of interest from under the bonnet, increasing in a linear fashion to 3500. Hit four grand, and the world's a beautiful place. The GT-R's accelerative prowess from this point to 6500 rpm is phenomenal, forcing an invisible hand against your chest and sending your left hand to the gear lever anticipating quick fire upshifts.

The six roars with heavy induction, then howls as it sprints athletically through a mid-range that dares the driver to push on. It's muffled, for sure, but you can hear and *feel* the Skyline race car. The engine has a sharp edged note that tears at the ears and pricks something deep and instinctive within anyone whose love for cars transcends plastic wheel trims and stick-on Garfield toys.

With the full 205 kW quota marching in at 6800 rpm, the 24 valve Nissan six steams on to the indicated 7450 rpm

redline. A noticeable drop-off in acceleration isn't evident once past the nominated power peak; in fact, the GT-R easily slides over the edge and on to a bed-of-nails limiter at a staggering 8200 rpm. That's big numbers for a production six and a testament to the engine's balance.

Bringing up the 400 metre mark in 13.7 secs, 100 km/h in 5.4 and 160 km/h in 13.8 was a Herculean effort, made partly possible by the ATESSA transmission configuration. Nissan says it based the GT-R around a rear drive layout, adding front drive simply to help out, not dominate. The static torque split is biased 100 per cent to the limited slip rear end. Once the rear breaks traction, the maximum value becomes 50 per cent rear and 50 per cent front. The amount of slip is closely monitored by a silicon brain that thinks in stereo, transferring drive front and rear depending on the grip balance. The GT-R's tendency to break the rear wheels free is a help when looking for maximum acceleration from rest, because it prevents the engine from bogging and falling off boost.

It's easy to be drawn into only admiring the Skyline GT-R's powerplant. Yes, it

The shift in weight combined with sudden lock application has a tendency to flick the GT-R into the corner. It's rare to approach that level of commitment and, when you do, the behaviour isn't unsettling or even vaguely disturbing, so reassuring is the Skyline's manner.

Nissan's sophisticated Super HICAS system works in two distinct steps; initially in reverse phase (with the rear wheels turning through a small arc in the opposite direction to the front) before moving to the parallel phase.

The steering is superb; there's no other word for it. On-road, its level of power assistance falls neatly between the two extremes and offers good feel around the centre. It's weighting is just right, and remains consistent no matter how far the steering wheel revolves through its 2.6 turns lock to lock. The system's accuracy and feel remain intact no matter what the road speed.

Ninety degree corners can be attacked a little more vigorously and here, the GT-R understeers initially and requires some thought to give its best. Mindlessly sink the boot, and the bespoilered Nissan runs wide then wider. Using throttle control to keep the line tight returns it to neutrality, and then the fun begins...

It's at this point that the turbos start to turn and, boy, you've got to hang on. Reminded of the car's speed on corner entry, the Skyline now delivers another impromptu sermon on acceleration. The

tail squats, revs rise at a ridiculous rate, and the tail steps out ... and *out*! Catch it with 180 degrees of steering lock, feather the throttle, and the Skyline voluntarily accepts the leash.

It's fast, alright, and it would be a bad mistake to underestimate the car's ability to cover ground. Technical advancement, after all, should never compromise a driver's sense of mortality. The key is, as always, slower in, faster out, anticipating boost on the exit, and keeping a consistent cornering speed, pulling boost in as early as possible.

Ride improves at these speeds, because the stiff calibration on springs and dampers copes better with the increased forces. The transmission, so sweet at low speeds, maintains the ease of shift and solid engagement that endeared it in the

NISSAN SKYLINE GT-R

GENERAL
Longitudinal front engine coupe, constant 4WD
List price $110,000

ENGINE
RB26DETT, twin turbocharged, intercooled in-line 6
Bore x stroke 86 x 74
Displacement 2568 cm^3
Compression ratio 8.5:1
Fuel system electronic fuel injection
Power 205 kW at 6800 rpm
Torque 355 Nm at 4400 rpm

TRANSMISSION
Five speed manual, ATESSA ET-S variable torque split 4WD
Gear ratios
First   3.214
Second   1.925
Third   1.302
Fourth   1.000
Fifth   0.752
Final drive   4.111

MEASUREMENTS
Length 4545 mm
Width 1755 mm
Height 1340 mm
Kerb weight 1530 kg
Fuel tank capacity 72 litres

SUSPENSION
Front: Multi-link, coils
Rear: Multi-link, coils

STEERING
Power assisted rack and pinion with Super HICAS 4WS

BRAKES
Four piston caliper vented discs/two piston caliper vented discs with anti-lock system

WHEELS & TYRES
Alloy 8JJ x 16
Bridgestone Potenza RE71 225/50R16 92V

PERFORMANCE
Standing start
0-60 km/h   2.2
0-80 km/h   3.8
0-100 km/h   5.4
0-120 km/h   7.8
0-140 km/h   10.4
0-160 km/h   13.8
0-400 metres 13.7
Rolling start

	3rd	4th	5th
40-70 km/h	4.4	6.9	11.4
60-90 km/h	3.4	5.6	10.3
80-110 km/h	3.2	4.7	5.7
100-130 km/h	3.5	4.5	7.3

first place. The speed of the shift seems to be inconsequential – Nissan's five-speeder will cope no matter how hurried the driver becomes.

Braking isn't as impressive. Fitted with an anti-lock system and massive ventilated rotors, the GT-R's anchors require a hefty prod on the centre pedal. They lack subtlety, preventing those incremental movements in the initial braking motion that make some stoppers so appealing. Pedal travel is short and makes heavy demands with little reward. Yes, they work; no, they're not in keeping with the GT-R's general ambience.

And ambience is the keyword in the conception of this car. Despite the GT-R's muscular machismo, its interior is a field of soft curves and even softer touches. Those bucket seats hang on tight and offer excellent support, but their appearance and material could have been formed from the action of water.

The shifter looks uncomfortable but slides smoothly into the palm. The dash is as integrated as the 300ZX's but more tasteful, offering well conceived binnacle controls with stubby knobs for lights and wipers. Instruments are clear and well positioned, but a number are probably there for sales purposes only. After all, it's hard to take in speedo, tacho, water

temperature, oil pressure, front axle torque, fuel level, turbo boost, oil temperature and volts in a single day...

Thankfully, Nissan sussed out the ergonomics, giving the wheel tilt *and* reach, and a dead pedal you can actually use without transmission tunnel intrusion. Rear leg room – this is, after all, a 2+2 – is surprisingly capacious. You couldn't call this a genuine four seat sedan, but it's certainly capable of carrying four adults for a reasonable distance without requiring medical attention.

Same goes for head room, which is excellent front and rear. Road noise becomes obtrusive across virtually any surface, caused by a combination of little noise abatement material (no doubt for weight) and considerable contact patches. And you don't have to be at warp speed for noise around the A pillar.

Putting the beast into perspective, there are very, very few people who will ever see its limits on a public road – the velocities the GT-R can comfortably sustain are simply beyond the realms of normal thinking (and driving) individuals. At $110,000, many will see it as frivolous and anti-social. Let them, because they won't see that the GT-R is a two-seater sports car inside a coupe body. Japan has put the meaning back into GT. ●

B L O WN
CHANCES

THESE ARE JAPAN'S ULTIMATE STREETFIGHTERS — TOYOTA'S REBORN, 211 kW, TWIN TURBO SUPRA AND THE MIGHTY NISSAN GT-R V-SPEC. BUT THEY WON'T BE OFFERED IN OZ BECAUSE THEIR MAKERS CAN'T SEE THE POINT. A MISSED OPPORTUNITY, WE RECKON. SO HERE IT IS, THE SAMURAI SHOWDOWN BETWEEN THE ONES THAT GOT AWAY . . .

BY PETER LYON
PHOTOGRAPHY BY RAY HASHIMOTO

A hot shot of adrenalin floods the veins as the new Supra's 3.0-litre twin turbos ignite. The word in motoring circles has been mixed, so the chance to test the new-comer for ourselves is all the more intriguing; not only that, this new Japanese streetfighter — along with its Nissan counterpart — won't be headed our way, having been halted by something even more powerful than themselves — the mighty Yen, which has put the cars out of contention for the Oz market on the sheer basis of price. So this is a special pairing, one to savour . . .

THE TRACTION CONTROL gets switched off because now isn't the time to worry about the cost of those fat rear tyres. Push the tacho past 4000 rpm, and smack — drop the clutch to unleash a weighty 211 kW of power. The mammoth 17-inch Bridgestone Potenzas fight vainly to hold traction; they howl then smoke, but once they grip, we're away and headed towards a 0-100 km/h time of just over five seconds. That's stinkingly quick in English, Japanese, or just about any other language you want to try. But is the final package everything chief engineer Isao Tsuzuki hoped for when he started working on the project eight long years ago? Ever since Nissan's state-of-the-art Group A-slaying Skyline GT-R came on to the scene back in 1989, Toyota has suffered something of an inferiority complex. After all, the GT-R was years ahead of its time. Toyota was Japan's number one carmaker, yet it didn't possess the top sports car. That hurt; Toyota had made a name for itself in motorsports events including Group C, Le Mans and in the World Rally Championship, but at home it had taken a back seat in the high performance sports car arena.

For Toyota, the new Supra had to be a better allrounder than its GT-R archrival and they did their darndest to achieve that goal, even stretching the normal four-year development cycle out to six.

Japan's wild bunch — the new Supra (FAR LEFT) and the Nissan GT-R V-spec (LEFT). The GT-R's exploits are well known, especially here in Australia — the only market outside Japan to offer the car — where it dominated touring car racing for a time. The Supra has a less illustrious record, but this model is a clear transformation of its predecessors, with power to burn (BELOW) . . .

In putting the new bad-ass on the block back-to-back with the Nissan fire-breather, other contenders were mentioned. Why not compare it with the other supercars that have unconditionally eclipsed the old Supra — one thinks immediately of the Honda NSX or Mazda RX-7? The answer is simple. Apart from the fact that the GT-R is the oldest and most proven of the wild bunch, it is also the only other Japanese sportscar to boast a similar in-line six cylinder twin turbo set-up generating 211 kW (not to be confused with the more powerful 239 kW US spec Supra), making it the only logical choice for this burn-out bonanza of a comparo.

The Supra, although a touch younger than the GT-R, has still managed to make a respectable name for itself since its 1979 debut. Unlike the GT-R which has maintained a common circular rear brake light design since its inception, and more recently sharper body panels, the fourth generation Supra's styling is as different from its predecessor as its performance.

Toyota's Nagoya HQ asked five design centres to submit ideas for the new Supra, including Calty in the US and Italdesign in Italy, to the Toyota Tokyo Design Centre and finally to the Supra team. With the US being the Supra's largest market, Calty pushed head office with its suggestion of a "Batmobile-like car" (the movie was breaking box office records at that time). Not

A little of the Ferrari F40 in the new Supra's styling; but the outsized rear wing is more than cosmetic, providing 45kg of downforce at 145/km/h. The in-line, sequential twin turbo six equals the GT-R's 211 kW output.

SUPRA

surprisingly, that idea was quickly shelved.

Supra stylists from HQ said they wanted a "uniquely Toyota design," but in doing so they ended up borrowing a number of styling cues from the Ferrari F40 — the shape of the grille, the trapezoidal headlights, and its colossal brake scoops, not to mention the huge rear wing, all pay homage to fastest prancing horse ever. But if Toyota were aiming to outdo Nissan in the rear wing department, they've certainly done it. The GT-R's spoiler, which once looked like a fairly aggressive piece of hardware, now looks rather sedate when put beside the Supra. However, it's not just cosmetic, says Toyota. The spoiler is claimed to provide 45kg of downforce at 145 km/h which is a welcome plus, especially when you've got the twin turbos in full flight entering a fast sweeper.

The overall Supra design could have been more aggressive, al-

though it does have more presence than its dated, Comaro-inspired predecessor. Sure, the Supra looks fast, with its 0.30 C_d — but hey, if you're going to create Japan's number one sportscar, you need some fangs for those jaws. It looks as if someone came up with a sharp design, and then someone else came along, stuck a straw into the body, and blew it up thus realising the bulbous shape you see now.

The GT-R's enormous front air dam, large boot mounted rear spoiler, bulging guards and neat side skirts provided an acceptably sporty look, although unfortunately its clumsy 0.40 C_d figure does not do justice to its race-proven performance.

Inside the car, Toyota designers wanted to keep things simple. The intention was honourable, but the result is a flat, featureless dash that appears to be too large and spartan, all designed to save

The GT-R V-spec retains the race-bred 2.6-litre in-line six cylinder engine with its twin ceramic turbochargers. Inside, the car is less spartan than the Supra, and has the advantage of a turbo boost gauge, which is surprisingly absent on the Toyota.

GT-R

weight. While it has a large tacho and speedo, other gauges seemingly necessary like a turbo boost dial are absent.

The expanse of black plastic on the dash, coupled with black leather seat coverings creates a slightly gloomy atmosphere, in a high waisted interior. The two-plus-two cabin layout caters well to the driver by way of high-backed supportive seats and excellent headroom, but the rear seats are for shopping or anklebiters only.

No weight saving measures were employed with the GT-R's cabin. The dash is more functional than the Supra's, and apart from the large centrally placed tacho and speedo, does feature such complimentary aids as a turbo boost gauge on the centre console.

The 1993 Supra shares its 3.0-litre 24-valve, in-line six with the Lexus SC300 and GS300. While the naturally aspirated version generates 164 kW at 5800 rpm, the Supra's two-way twin sequential turbos strapped on to the starboard flank muster an extra 47 kW and a whopping 431 Nm at 3600 rpm of torque. The smaller turbo spins up to full boost at around 2500 rpm, where the big brother kicks in for the big blow to the 6800 rpm redline.

The GT-R V-Spec meanwhile, retains its race-bred 2.6-litre, 24-valve, in-line six with two ceramic Garrett turbochargers and intercoolers controlling both fuel injection and ignition to produce a very potent 211 kW at 6800 rpm and 353 Nm at 4400rpm.

Both cars produce the same maximum power but the Toyota has the torque advantage. On the scales, there's only a 10 kg difference — the GT-R heavier at 1500 kg. So the weight to power ratio turns out to be almost identical at 7.06 kg/kW for the Supra and 7.11 kg/kW for the GT-R. But what does all that mean in terms of performance? Is the Supra able to transfer that slight weight/power advantage to the road, remembering of course that the Toyota only has two wheels driven compared with the GT-R's four?

PERFORMANCE

Performance figures very soon told the story. Even the Supra's massive 255/40ZR-17 tyres could not provide the kind of traction necessary to get the power down on to the road, whereas the GT-R V-Spec's superior combination of new 17-inch tyres and all-paws traction won out on all the major sprint tests. It was faster up to 100 km/h (5.10 seconds plays 5.21 seconds), and comfortably faster over the standing 400m (12.58 to 13.51) as well as the standing 1km, but could not manage the highest top speed, which went to the Supra with 250 km/h.

What we need to point out, though, is that the 239 kW US-spec Supra has stopped the clocks at a blistering 4.6 seconds for the bolt to 100 km/h, but Japanese transport ministry regulations restrict the maximum power output of domestic sportscars to 211 kW.

Four years down the track since its release, the GT-R has come in for some worthwhile refinements, and now goes under the new title of GT-R V-Spec. These changes include larger 17-inch BBS aluminium wheels and Bridgestone Potenza tyres, and, for the first time on a Japanese production car, Italy's Brembo racing brakes have been employed. This specially designed brake package features large-area racing calipers, and larger 324 mm front discs and 300 mm rear discs. The previously heavy-weight clutch pedal has been lightened and the electronically-controlled torque split 4wd ATTESA E-TS system has had some fine-tuning refinements.

We punished both cars around the Tsukuba race course north of Tokyo, and it didn't take long for the GT-R to consolidate the superiority it had demonstrated in a straight line. It's average lap time of 1 minute 6.19 seconds overshadowed the Supra's 1 minute 9.16 seconds, and was testament to the GT-R's claim to the Japanese sportscar hall of fame.

But what about on the road? Our test over the winding mountain roads south of Tokyo sorted that out. But before we get into the handling department we need to briefly mention how the cars have been set-up for maximum forward motion.

The GT-R V-spec has retuned ATTESA ETS (Advanced Total Traction Engineering System for All Terrains and Electronic Torque Split) to cater for the wider 17 inch tyres. It's unique among production four-wheel drive systems, as it employs an accelerator to detect lateral or sideways movement, and adjusts the torque split accordingly between front and rear wheels in the op-

posite direction to those at the front before switching back the other way to run in unison.

Four-wheel drive and four-wheel steer were initially considered by Supra's engineering team, but were deemed "unnecessary technology" in that it would have added unwanted lard. In an age of continuously fighting to outmanoeuvre your rival's mechanical advances, this move sideways is most refreshing, even if Nissan has managed to pack it in yet remain almost identical on the scales.

With 211 kW of power being force-fed to the Supra's rear wheels, the stability and refinement of the chassis becomes crucial. The car's structure is much stiffer than the old Supra, despite being 140 kg lighter. The Supra shares a modified version of the

Lexus SC300's platform, shortened by 14 cm, with extensive revisions to the overall geometry. Front suspension is independent by unequal length control arms with coil springs and anti-roll bars. On the rear, it's independent by semi-trailing arms with lateral links, coil springs and anti-roll bars.

Even with the wide 255/40ZR-17 Bridgestone Potenzas fitted to the rear, it doesn't require too much effort to give a road surface the black stripe treatment. To temper the Supra's hooligan character, Tsuzuki employed a traction control system that limits an oversupply of power and torque to the back end.

With this in play, we hit the road. Getting up to speed in the Supra required little effort, thanks to the sequential twin turbos which turn the Toyota straight six into a true muscle car engine. Pushing the tacho up to its 6800 rpm redline in second, the needle caressed the 100 km/h mark before we went into third. Under heavy acceleration, the Supra generates a deep, gruff exhaust note that sounds exhilarating both inside and outside the car.

The 24-valve six really gets into stride around 3500 rpm, at which point the turbos are singing freely and producing seemingly boundless energy. It's difficult not to be impressed by the engine's deep seam of torque and eager response when the blowers are spooled up. The gearbox has been stacked to provide a nice even spread between the six ratios, and used sensibly, the engine need never drop out of the peak torque band. Yet it's possible to sit on 50 km/h in sixth at 1000 rpm and still have workable acceleration on tap.

Considering the amount of power to play with, the Supra's gearbox is surprisingly light and flickable. The throws are short and well matched in effort by the clutch pedal.

Staying around 100 km/h we negotiated our first "three figure" corner. Plenty of throttle induced oversteer here, but if you run shy, simply lift off even at mid-turn. The tail tucks in nicely and the drama subsides. In comparison to another rear wheel drive turbo, the RX-7, the Supra doesn't suffer from the almost uncontrollable lashings of power oversteer that can make the Mazda a real driving challenge. And it isn't plagued by the slight turbo lag apparent in the RX-7 — Tsuzuki pointed out that the new Supra turbo is designed to be inherently stable, with a just a slight emphasis on oversteer.

On the other hand, the GT-R V-Spec, said in motoring circles to be the best handling car out of Japan, still seems to hold the title. It may be a much higher revving engine, but its phenomenal ability to get its awesome power down on to the road has been further enhanced by the new combination of 225/50RZ-17 Bridgestone Potenzas tyres and the retuned ATTESA 4wd system.

The GT-R glides through turns with a minimum of fuss, all four wheels providing maximum grip and almost no oversteer. The GT-R feels much safer at the limits of adhesion than the Supra, simply due to the GT-R's incomparable 4wd system.

Yet another modification to the GT-R which gave it an edge is the Brembo racing brake package.

The pizza-like 324 mm front discs and 300 mm rear discs couple with race-bred calipers and brake rotors and a four channel ABS system to give the GT-R even more superiority, allowing you to leave braking to the absolute last fraction of a second before entering a corner.

The Supra brakes are also excellent, but are eclipsed when compared with such a purpose-built racing brake package. The Toyota sports 322 mm front discs and massive 325 mm rear discs, along with unusual spiral ventil-action brake cooling fins and a four-channel anti-lock braking system.

No complaints here. Plenty of stopping power, but the feel through the pedal and the ultimate level of retardation is a win to the Nissan.

	Nissan Skyline GT-R V-spec 2.6-litre 5-sp manual	Toyota Supra 3.0-litre, 6-sp manual
ENGINE		
Location	front, longitudinally mounted	front, longitudinally mounted
Cylinders	six, in-line	six, in-line
Bore x stroke	86.0 x 73.7 mm	86.0 x 86.0 mm
Capacity	2568 cm³	2997 cm³
Induction	electronic multi-point fuel injection twin turbochargers	electronic multi-point fuel injection, twin turbochargers
Compression ratio	8.5:1	8.5:1
Valve gear	cog-belt driven ohc four valves/cyl	cog-belt driven double ohc four valves/cyl
Power	211 kW @ 6800 rpm	211 kW @ 5600 rpm
Torque	353 Nm @ 4400 rpm	422 Nm @ 3600 rpm

GEARBOX						
Gear	ratio	km/h 1000 rpm	Max Speed	At (rpm)	ratio	km/h 1000 rpm	Max Speed	At (rpm)
First	3.214	9.0	72	8000	3.830	9.8	67	6800
Second	1.925	15.0	120	8000	2.360	16.0	109	6800
Third	1.302	22.1	177	8000	1.690	22.3	152	6800
Fourth	1.000	28.7	230	8000	1.310	28.8	196	6800
Fifth	0.752	27.3	219	5700	1.000	38.9	249	6400
Sixth					0.790	48.0	250	5200
Final-Drive	4.11				3.08			
Driving wheels	four				rear			

SUSPENSION		
Front	Independent by multi-link, unequal length arms with coil springs and anti-roll bar	independent by unequal length arms with coil springs and anti-roll bar
Rear	Independent by multi-link, with coil springs and anti-roll bar	independent by semi-trailing arm with lateral links, coil springs and anti-roll bar
Wheels	alloy 8.0 JJ x 17	alloy 8.0 JJ x 17 f 9.55 JJ x 17 r
Tyres	Bridgestone Potenza 225/50 ZR 17	Bridgestone Potenza 235/45 ZR 17 f 255/40 ZR 17 r

BRAKES		
Front	ventilated 324 mm discs	ventilated 322 mm discs
Rear	ventilated 300 mm discs	325 mm discs
Anti-lock	yes	yes

STEERING		
Type	power assisted rack and pinion	power assisted rack and pinion

DIMENSIONS (mm)		
Wheelbase	2615	2550
Front track	1480	1520
Rear track	1480	1525
Overall length	4545	4520
Overall width	1755	1810
Overall height	1355	1275
Ground clearance	140	130
Kerb weight (kg)	1500	1490
Weight to power (kg/kW)	5.36	5.32
Fuel tank (l)	72.0	70.0

ACCELERATION (seconds)		
0-100 km/h	5.10	5.21
Standing 400m	12.58 seconds	13.51 seconds
Standing km	24.51 seconds	25.16 seconds

For Australians the shoot-out between the Supra and the GT-R is a story of missed opportunity. With the possible exception of the Honda NS-X, these two cars are Japan's greatest sporting triumphs, and when the day-to-day considerations are thrown in — visibility, comfort, refinement, ventilation, ease of operation — they're as desirable as just about anything in the world. For Australia to miss out on this pair really is a tragedy.

However the question of a victor still needs to be answered, and the bottom line is that in this Japanese spec at least, the GT-R still rules.

The Supra may be the fresher of the two, but old Godzilla still has it measure for grunt, grip, handling finesse, and stopping power. The king lives on. **M**

KILLER

It's a beast with a brain – combining high-tech engineering and old-fashion

Godzilla's back! And it's meaner than ever. Fully 18 months after the launch of the all-new Skyline range in Japan, cash-strapped Nissan has finally unveiled the successor to one of the world's finest sports coupes.

The good news is that Godzilla II is quicker than ever – Nissan insiders claim standing 400m times in the mid-13 second bracket and say the new car has lapped Nurburgring 21 seconds faster than the old one. The bad news is that Nissan is still dithering over whether to export its Porsche crushing supercar.

Its tortuous evolution hints at the turmoil within Nissan, which is still reeling from the collapse in sales and profits following the bursting of Japan's bubble economy.

And its dimensions – longer, wider, taller and heavier than the old car – are not clever in a business where, increasingly, smart car companies are finding less is more.

The reason is not sloppiness on the part of the GT-R engineering team, but cost – instead of having a unique platform, the Skyline range is now built on the same underpinnings as the larger, heavier, more luxurious Laurel (a Cressida

GODZILLA!

tention to detail. ANGUS MacKENZIE and PETER NUNN appraise Nissan's brutal beauty

competitor in Japan) to save money. That's why the new GT-R is 130 mm longer overall and rolls on a 105 mm longer wheelbase.

Nissan previewed the new GT-R alongside the rest of the Skyline range at the 1993 Tokyo Show. Every panel is brand new, though Godzilla II's styling is clearly evolutionary rather than revolutionary. The muscular bulges over the wheelarches and dual afterburner tail-lights are familiar Skyline call signs. Since Tokyo, Nissan has also rejigged the front grille and bumper assembly, and added a race-style four way adjustable rear wing.

Nissan claims the wing, the deep front spoiler and the subtle side skirts help the new GT-R achieve a Cd of 0.35, compared with the brick-like 0.40 of the old car. Not that you could tell the difference hot lapping the Ginza...

To boost body rigidity, Nissan has added braces front and rear to tie the suspension strut towers together, a stiffening panel behind the rear seats, crossbars in a thicker floorpan, larger cross section centre pillars and stronger sills. The extra steel accounts in part for the GT-R's 1530 kg kerb weight – up 100 kg on the old car – but Nissan has tried to make amends by stamping the bonnet and front guards in aluminium. The saving? 12 kg.

All new though eerily familiar, Godzilla II's interior has a new dash, new instrument binnacle – with fake carbon fibre around the dials – and a new airbag steering wheel. But the presentation of the centre console, with its three auxiliary gauges – boost, oil temperature and torque split – and sound system pack, looks almost identical to that of the old car. You can have it in any colour you want – as long as it's dark grey.

If you want a real *deja view*, however, just lift the bonnet. The mighty 2.6 litre twin turbo RB26DETT in-line six looks like it has been lifted straight out of the old car – which is basically what happened.

Skyline GTB, 1966

Original Skyline GT-R, 1969

Godzilla II's styling is evolutionary. The muscular bulges over th

There's a new oil filler cap, and a beautifully crafted race-style adjustable brace anchoring the front strut towers. But otherwise the engine bay is identical, right down to the graphics on the cam cover and plenum chamber.

Nissan claims the engine delivers the same power – 206 kW at 6800 rpm – as in the old car, but is unlikely to advertise an increase for fear of violating the Japanese industry's agreement to limit production car outputs to 221 kW.

The factory says the new car's extra performance comes from a three per cent increase in torque to 367 Nm at 4400 rpm, new lightweight ceramic turbochargers which enable the engine to spin more rapidly to the redline – and a trick new computerised four-wheel drive system which boosts traction.

The system is a development of the existing ATESSA E-TS electronically variable torque split transmission, which varies the amount of torque fed to the front wheels from zero to 50 per cent, depending on data from sensors monitoring vehicle speed and lateral force.

In simple terms, the car is set up as a rear-wheel drive, with torque being progressively fed to the front wheels as the rears break traction.

In the old car the system produced prodigious grunt out of corners with little of the understeer normally associated with four-wheel drive.

Former HRT driver Win Percy described it this way after a session with the car at Eastern Creek: "The initial turn-in is good, but until you've got the confidence it feels as though it's going to understeer quite badly.

"Through tight corners you can get the power on a darned sight earlier than in a two-wheel drive car. By playing on the racetrack, you can get the front-wheel

The Skyline's The Limit

PRINCE MOTORS LAUNCHED the original Skyline in 1956 as a 1.5 litre four door featuring a de Dion rear axle, quite an unusual feature for a mid-'50s Japanese car wrapped in an unadventurous body. It evolved into the big Nissan Gloria. Though part of Nissan today, Prince Motors started out as a spin-off of Nakajima Aircraft – another, larger offshoot became Fuji Heavy Industries, maker of Subaru.

The second Skyline, in 1964, introduced an alternator, 54 kW ohc four cylinder engine and optional front disc brakes to the Japanese mass market – and was the basis for the GT-R's *real* ancestor, the original Skyline GT. Under the auspices of Skyline program manager S. Sakurai, the car was chopped off at the cowl, 200 mm grafted in for a longer engine bay and a 2.0 litre Gloria ohc six slipped in.

Sakurai swapped the Gloria's single carby for a set of triple Webers, which boosted output to a then astonishing 95 kW, and *voila!* – Japan's first performance sedan, which was shipped to Australia in small but significant numbers.

Prince, by then owned by Nissan, went ahead with the third generation Skyline (again under Sakurai-san). The debut Skyline GT-R carried Japan's first four valve twin cam, a 2.0 litre six reputed to develop at least 25 kW more than the 'official' 125 kW rating. The GT-R was launched as a four door, but in 1970 a short wheelbase two door hardtop was supplying the basis for the hottest (and most successful) of Japan's touring cars. In 1973 Sakurai and company popped a third generation GT-R (based on the 240K two door hardtop), the last of the line for some time.

The now legendary 1990 Godzilla was the handiwork of a team headed by program manager K. Watanabe. The latest bowed under S. Itoh and seems to work as well as the original – so, we assume, does the development group.   **BOB HALL**

Skyline GT-R hardtop, 1971

Skyline GT-R, 1973

wheel arches and dual afterburner tail-lights are familiar Skyline call signs

Niche and Nasty: 'Just Do It'

Australia was the only market in the world outside Japan where the previous GT-R was sold with full compliance and warranty. But that's no guarantee we'll get the new model, according to Nissan insiders. Nissan Japan steadfastly refuses to develop the GT-R for export, despite performance and handling which put it among major league supercars. This curiously myopic attitude robs Nissan of the potential to use the GT-R as a niche image builder, the way BMW uses the glorious M3 coupe.

The previous GT-R arrived in Australia because then Nissan Australia chief Ivan Deveson brought in a limited number of road cars to support the company's on-track activities with Fred Gibson's works-backed GT-R race team.

Marketing guys liked the idea; finance guys, who'd been told the program might just break even, hated it. In the end, says former Nissan chief engineer Don Dunoon, it came down to Deveson simply saying "do it".

Dunoon went to Japan, figured the GT-R could be adapted to meet ADRs, and persuaded the Japanese to agree. "Their attitude was very strange," he recalls. "They gave me some cars, but basically said 'we don't want to know'."

Dunoon's small team embarked on a six month ADR program. The budget was a modest $250,000. The first thing they did was disconnect the 180 km/h speed limiter. Running the GT-R flat out for sustained periods revealed shortcomings: the diff, gearbox and transfer case oil temperatures all soared. A special transmission oil cooler was one of 250 changes the Australians made to meet ADR and durability targets.

Other changes included side intrusion bars, new muffler and windscreen, changes to the instrument panel, and a complete rejig of the rear lights.

Dunoon also wanted 17 inch wheels and bigger brakes – both features of Godzilla II. Head office engineers had components on the shelf but the marketing department said no. "It's the one area where we could really have made the car better," he says.

Nissan Japan was also persuaded to batch build all 100 GT-Rs destined for Australian in one hit, complete with the Australian spec windscreen and muffler. Each GT-R then required a further 50 hours of work at Nissan's Clayton plant before being released to dealers to fit intrusion bars and tail-lights, among other tasks.

With Nissan Australia now merely an importer, ADR compliance work would have to be done in Japan. This would push the GT-R's pricetag to $190,000 by the time it reached Australia, almost 75 per cent more than the old car.

The price wouldn't scare off Kevin Jarrett, pictured, who has logged 25,000 km in his two-year-old GT-R. It has been utterly reliable in both daily driving and hot laps of Oran Park. Having owned Porsches and Ferraris, he reckons there's no better high performance buy. "I don't know what I'd replace it with, apart from the new GT-R."

ANGUS MacKENZIE

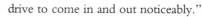

drive to come in and out noticeably."

For the new car, Nissan has linked the ATTESA system with a new yaw-rate feedback Super HICAS four-wheel steering for more finely tuned cornering responses. The system first estimates vehicle motion corresponding to the driver's intentions from changes in wheel speed and steering angle.

At the same time, a sensor feeds the yaw rate back to the computer controlling the system for comparison with pre-programmed target values. The computer then adjusts the rear wheel steer angle. Nissan claims the system enhances stability on rough roads and at high speed.

Other upgrades to chassis hardware include the adoption of Brembo brakes all round and detail improvements to the multi-link suspension. The upper link of the front suspension is now a two arm fabrication for increased camber stiffness. Rear suspension travel has been increased to improve tyre contact with the road.

Massive 17 inch alloys – up one inch from the old car – now run lower, wider 245/45ZR tyres.

But wait, there's more: range topping V spec GT-Rs get the new ATTESA E-TS PRO system which integrates control of the driving and braking forces on all four wheels independently.

Key to this system is a computer controlled limited-slip diff which combines with the four-wheel drive and steering

electronics to ensure optimum traction under all conditions. V spec cars also get stiffer spring and damper rates for even better on-the-limit handling.

Such high technology chassis engineering combined with good old-fashioned attention to detail – Nissan even moved the battery to the boot to improve weight distribution – rather than a big increase in horsepower gives the new Skyline GT-R the edge over its illustrious predecessor.

Nissan quotes a standing 400m time of 13.5 seconds – running two up, with a full tank of fuel, at an ambient of 25 degrees C. That's a full 0.4 ses quicker than the factory quoted time for the old car – and 0.2 secs under the time *Wheels* Correvit time in 1990. The queue starts here...

Famous Skyline

Boyd Harnell and John Trent on the Skyline GTR V-Spec, Nissan's new home-market flagship.

In Japan's 1994 racing wars a team of modified Nissan Skyline GTRs blew away the rest of the field to win all eight events and a pair of championship titles. This enviable record came through the successful synthesis of some widely disparate automotive technologies, with Nissan molding and shaping all the latest ideas of Japan, Inc. into a single lightning-fast, highly responsive, monstrously rigid coupe.

The progeny of this victorious competitor is the newly redesigned 1995 Skyline GTR V-Spec for the street, which boasts a long-overdue restyle in addition to its upgraded performance. The new body hunkers lower and wider than before and the gorgeously retrostyle rear spoiler is now adjustable to four angles of attack. (Not incidentally, the GTR's drag figure has also dropped from last year's embarrassing .40 Cd to a fair-enough .35.) It's still no head-turning styling showcase, but the understated lines are at least in keeping with the GTR's long history of visual restraint.

Under the hood is where one really finds the GTR's soul; here lies a sleeping tiger. Nissan has reworked the 24-valve inline-6 by increasing compression, readjusting timing, raising turbo boost, remapping the control software and improving the intercooler efficiency. The resulting V-Spec

engine boasts a claimed—but certainly conservative—280 bhp @ 6800 rpm and an equally pessimistic 271 lbs.-ft. of torque. Some turbo lag besets the 2.6-liter mill under 3000 revs, but after that comes only a smooth explosion of power—enough to launch the car to 60 faster than an F355.

After sliding into the monofoam bucket seat you're greeted by a sensible array of analog gauges, all of them well within view and directly related to the V-Spec's primary functions. Amenities such as air conditioning and a stereo/CD are optional, though the hardcore enthusiast might forego these pleasures in the interest of weight reduction—after all, Nissan has recast the Skyline's front fenders and hood in aluminum to shave off an additional 26 pounds.

After weaving madly through Tokyo's infamous traffic I set a course for a new low-volume bypass road that runs far beyond the city. When the coast finally proved clear I set up the timing gear, ran the tach to six grand and popped the clutch. The GTR leapt forward, and I quickly slammed into second before the rev limiter could cut off the power at 8000 rpm. Smooth, powerful turbo boost and the surefooted traction of a sophisticated all-wheel-drive system carried the V-Spec up to 100 kph—62.5 mph—just as I finished my shift into third. Despite a couple of mistakes on my part during this initial run the timer still confirmed a 4.6-second blast.

Just as impressively, the GTR tracks straight as an arrow while acquiring speed and feels completely at ease in scrubbing it back off. Its 4-wheel discs use the same pads, rotors and calipers as many of today's IMSA racers, and while some racetrack tests have found brake fade even in this impressive hardware I could generate none—not on the road and not at our private testing course near Tama City.

The Tama course's twisting series of mostly uncambered curves was easily managed by the GTR's real-time electronic traction control system. At speed the V-Spec still shows a hint of understeer on harsher corners—a longtime Skyline GTR trait—but overall its cornering prowess is impressive, with minimal body roll and supreme adhesion as the orders of the day. While much of the V-Spec's superior handling can be attributed to Nissan's well proven Super-HICAS 4-wheel steering, that's just the beginning. Tied into the Super-HICAS this year is a yaw-rate feedback system that deduces the driver's intentions via sensors monitoring the vehicle's actual yaw rate, the driver's steering inputs and independent wheel speeds. Preprogrammed target values are then compared with the actual data coming into the system and discrepancies are corrected via the precise degree of rear-wheel-steering.

This complex wizardry also ties into the car's ATTESA-TS PRO all-wheel-drive

system, which boasts active electronic control of its center differential and limited-split rear diff. Effectively, these gadgets allow the V-Spec to continually redistribute torque from front to rear and left to right in addition to altering the relationship of the front and rear slip angles via the 4WS. All heady stuff if the computer can handle it.

Of course, the purely mechanical aspects of the V-Spec's suspension system help considerably, too. The multilink rear has been tweaked to provide more constant contact with the road and the front suspension's geometry gains camber stiffness to assist its turn-in precision. These efforts succeed, for turn-in is now immediate, rapid lane changes have virtually no effect on stability and high-speed tracking proves flawless.

Model-specific Bridgestone Expedias on unique alloy wheels round out the handling package, but this rubber's low profile only contributes to the GTR's harsh ride over less-than-perfect surfaces. Though never quite jarring, the Skyline does transmit a good bit of jounce and thump into the passenger compartment.

Nissan has taken stiffening almost to the point of overkill, by installing strut-tower bars front and rear, a separate crossbar up front with another under the floor and three more at the back, a shear panel behind the rear seats and steel door beams.

I'd have loved more seat time in the GTR to have further explored these changes, but Nissan's home-market press flaks—despite their plummeting

domestic and overseas sales—have slapped a new 2-day restriction on this car. This ridiculous policy mandated a second 2-day session merely to finish SCI's performance testing and photography, so the GTR's abilities as a traveling car or an everyday conveyance will have to be left in question—perhaps intentionally, considering its harshness over rough pavement.

Regardless, rather than ending on that sour note I'm still inclined to compliment Nissan's engineers on accomplishing a masterpiece in this latest GTR. It's an exhilarating experience on the road, and certainly worth the $70,000 or so one must shell out to own it. The hitch for Americans, of course, is that it's only available in its land of manufacture. ●

SPECIFICATIONS

1995 Nissan Skyline GTR V-Spec

General
Vehicle type: front-engine AWD coupe
Structure: steel unibody with steel and aluminum outer panels
Market as tested: Japan
MSRP: $69,500
Airbag: std., driver and passenger

Engine
Type: longitudinal L6, iron block and aluminum head
Displacement (cc): 2568
Compression ratio: 8.5:1
Power (bhp): 280* @ 6800 rpm
Torque (lbs. ft.): 272* @ 4400 rpm
Intake system: SMPFI with two intercooled turbochargers
Valvetrain: two overhead cams, four valves per cylinder

Transmission
Type: 5-speed manual
Ratios
1st: 3.21
2nd: 1.93
3rd: 1.30
4th: 1.00
5th: 0.75
Final drive: 4.11

Dimensions
Curb weight (lbs.): 3366
Wheelbase (in.): 107.1
Length (in.): 184.1
Width (in.): 70.1

Suspension, brakes, steering
Suspension, front: multilink with coil springs and antiroll bar
Suspension, rear: multilink with coil springs and antiroll bar
Steering type: rack and pinion, power assisted
Tires: 245/45ZR17
Brakes, f/r: 12.6-inch vented disc/11.7-inch vented disc
ABS: std.

Performance
0-60 (sec.): 4.4
1/4 mile (sec.): 12.7
Top speed (mph): 112 (electronically limited)

*factory rating

Ode to a Skyline

We test Nissan's wildest car— the Skyline GT-R V-Spec—on its home turf, and get a wing clipped, too.

BY DON SCHROEDER

Saturday, 9 a.m., Hakone, Japan: After two days of rounding up test cars beneath gray skies, it's our first sunny day. We stop at a Cosmo service station for a fill-up and a carwash. In contrast to the good ol' U.S., here stations are stocked with cheerful, eager-to-please attendants who apparently have not heard the term "chump change."

The Supra Turbo is parked in the bay of a "Lugar Big Top," a car-washing superstructure that moves on rails back and forth over the parked car. The Big Top completes its motion to the rear of the Supra, then stops abruptly. The control-panel lights blink urgently: the rear brush is stuck behind the Supra's wild rear wing, a $500 option.

One smiling attendant, 20-year-old Miss Motoko Yoshikawa, marches confidently over to the control panel, ponders it for a moment, and presses a button. The Big Top lurches forward and rips off the Supra's rear wing with a sickening crackling noise, that same sound you remember as a kid perching on a tree limb just before it collapsed.

This causes pandemonium at the station. Attendants and the manager run over, yelling and gesticulating wildly. Yoshikawa-san has crouched on the ground, head in her hands, and is weeping.

The good news is it wasn't the Nissan Skyline GT-R, the subject of this test. Skylines are a line of sporty coupes and sedans sold only in Japan and Australia. That, in itself, is not a good enough reason to go to Japan to test one. The 1995 GT-R version's turbocharged 2.6-liter in-line six, its four-wheel-drive, its considerable racing history, and the fact that it is a new version of Nissan's most sophisticated performance car constitute considerably better reasons. To put the GT-R in proper context, we rounded up two standards we know well— a Toyota Supra Turbo and a Corvette.

Seven easy steps . . .

. . . to customizing your Supra.

Between them, these Japanese Gen-Xers own three generations of GT-Rs.

The predecessor to this car appeared in 1989, the year Nissan cooked up the first twin-turbo and intercooled 4wd Skyline for Group A and N track racing. Enthusiasts around the world salivated over its technology, as did we when we test-drove a GT-R that had been sneaked into the U.S. and tweaked to about 350 horsepower. We called it "so good, it's scary."

The new GT-R appeared in January. It comes in three forms: standard GT-R; the GT-R V-Spec you see here, which has a more advanced driveline; and a racing version with a revised suspension, called the N1.

In any form, the new GT-R is technically peerless. For motivation, twin ceramic turbochargers with an intercooler feed a 2.6-liter six with 12.0 psi of boost. The claimed 276 hp (at 6800 rpm) bumps up against the Japanese automakers' voluntary power ceiling (Nissan insiders say the GT-R's actual figure is more like 311 hp). At 4400 rpm, there's 271 pound-feet of

torque. Redline is a sizzling 8000 rpm.

A five-speed manual feeds the GT-R's four-wheel drive via a center differential sporting an electronically controlled multiplate clutch. This "ATTESA E-TS" system sends 100 percent of the torque to the rear wheels until a wheel sensor detects slip—then it meters up to 50 percent of the torque to the front. Our V-Spec GT-R had *yet another* electronically controlled clutch, called A-LSD, which serves as a separate limited-slip differential for the rear wheels. The intent of this complexity is to distribute just the right amount of torque to each wheel to provide neutral handling, not simply maximum full-time traction.

Massive 245/45ZR-17 Bridgestone Expedias on alloy wheels are controlled by unequal-length control arms up front, with control arms and links in the rear on their own subframe. The final piece of the puzzle is Nissan's electronically controlled Super HICAS rear-wheel steering, which now

receives information from a new yaw sensor installed in the trunk.

Sunday, 11 a.m., Hakone: We're at a crowded snack bar at an intersection of the Ashino-ko Skyline, a meticulously maintained collection of curves, sweepers, and switchbacks making up a scenic road surrounding Hakone's Lake Ashi. The traditional Japanese breakfast looks just like last night's dinner; Pat Bedard once described it as "a do-it-yourself fish assembly kit." It just hasn't hit the spot, so we're now furtively wolfing down food we recognize—coffee, Oreos, and Pocky-Sticks, which are Japanese junk food in the form of little chocolate-coated pretzels.

In the parking lot are hundreds of sport motorcycles—all the Japanese marques, with dozens of Ducatis, BMWs, and new Triumphs mixed in. Our correspondent, Yasushi Ishiwatari, calls their riders, none of whom look older than 18, "mountain road boys." They wear brightly colored leathers tattooed with mangled English.

An example is a jacket with a big red cross and the words:

> *Yellow Corn*
> *Sledgehammer*
> *Highway the Third*

A cross on a biker jacket seems like good insurance, considering the treacherous roads. The lanes are narrow, passing zones plentiful, and warning signs few. But most spooky are the curves, which are lined with sharp-edged, eight-inch-deep concrete drainage ditches, ready to catch a wheel or rip out a suspension. The mountain road boys aren't known for reckless driving, but then again the ambulances around here are busy around the clock on weekends.

On these roads, the Supra Turbo is just as we remember in the States: cool and composed, with naturally weighted steering, progressive responses, and smooth, consistent thrust from its twin-turbocharged 276-hp 3.0-liter six. Its sharp, unfettered handling allows you to cut each curve and corner into consistent and manageable bite-sized chunks: brake, turn-in, and back on the throttle. Repeat.

If the Supra is a Japanese ceramic knife, the Corvette is a backwoodsman's axe: big, brutal, undoubtedly effective. The 300-hp 5.7-liter V-8 dominates this car, even occasionally manhandling the suspension. Our car, like most Japanese-specification Corvettes, was equipped with the base shocks and springs, which can get floaty and restless under the narcotic influence of the LT1's heady torque curve. Smooth inputs are required to keep the Vette on the straight and narrow, but there's more than enough tire grip, braking, and power to get the job done.

Take the Corvette's grip and the Supra Turbo's precision, add benign and neutral four-wheel drive, and you've got a GT-R. This car is great fun, leaping from corner to corner with the kind of sticky pull behind the wheel that we've seen with four-wheel-drivers like the Mitsubishi 3000GT VR4 and Porsche 911 Turbo. The soundtrack resembles that of a slightly

Some expat American cars in Japan—Corvettes included—are saddled with ungainly fender flares. Plus, there are the difficulties of being left-handed in a right-hand-drive world, evidenced here at one of Japan's many tollbooths.

Left: In crowded Tokyo, streetlight poles often protrude into your lane. Avoiding them and cyclists makes for slow progress during rush hour: we went six miles in four hours. Below: The Supra Turbo flirts with sharp-edged drainage ditch on an Ashi-no-ko Skyline hairpin.

Left: Lunch stop means eggs hard-boiled in hot springs on Mount Kamiyama, a 3000-year-old active volcano. The hydrochloric and sulfuric acids in Kamiyama's scalding waters stain the eggs in unearthly shades of beige and black. Above: Wide-load Vette felt unwieldy under full power on Japan's narrow roads.

muffled BMW M5—an urgent, insistent droning from underhood.

From our somewhat tired press car (with 7000 miles on the clock), we could still extract 60 mph in 5.3 seconds and a quarter-mile time of 14.0 seconds at 104 mph. (Japanese magazines recorded much faster times, but their uncorrected testing was done in the winter cold, with launches that allowed spinning rear tires.) A GT-R in better shape than ours would certainly get to 60 mph in under five seconds. Still, our GT-R's speed is in a dead heat with the Vette's and Supra Turbo's until 113 mph, where a Japan-standard

governor abruptly halts the fun.

The GT-R's 0.94-g roadholding may be the most usable grip since evolution stumbled upon the opposable thumb. The driveline technology controls power-on oversteer expertly—avoid overcooking the entry speed in a turn and you'll make like F1's Ukyo Katayama every time. On a track, the GT-R is magnificent: brake just deep enough into a corner to slide the tail, get on the gas early to crank up the boost, and the ATTESA system feeds in just enough front torque to rein in the oversteer and explode the GT-R out of the corner.

Tuesday, 3 p.m., Tokyo: One hour in Tokyo rush-hour traffic can make Los Angeles seem like Tulsa. But Tokyo drivers remain courteous, even in the face of driving habits that westerners would find infuriating. The turn signal is used by many drivers as an all-purpose device, when they want to slow down and park anywhere—adjacent to another car, at a corner, or blocking a lane on a busy thoroughfare. That might light off an explosion of horns in New York City, but we heard only one horn in Tokyo—blown at me, in fact, as I nearly caused an accident trying to wheedle the $55,200 GT-R around one *of those random parkers. Before you laugh, remember that the rear-view mirrors and blind spots on a right-hand-drive car are reversed.*

A $55,200 pricetag doesn't make the GT-R exclusive. In three days, we saw at least a dozen of them, many driven by guys more in the market for Clearasil than Barbasol. Nissan says that in a six-month period last year, fully one-quarter of GT-R buyers were under the age of 25, and that trend continues. Who are these guys? Trust-fund babies? Drug dealers? (Nah.) Yakuza? (Maybe.)

Remember, this is a country where the average full-time worker makes about a third more than the average U.S. worker—at least $45,000 a year. Despite the pay scale, real estate remains beyond the reach of many, freeing up yen for other expenditures. Fancy cars, for one. Some banks in Japan still don't require comprehensive insurance to back up expensive car loans, because default rates are low. Many hotshoes in Japan, says Ishiwatari, are paying off two or three loans but driving only one car. The other two were balled up on roads like the Ashi-no-ko Skyline.

Balling up a GT-R would be very sad. This is a handsome car—not as neatly tailored as its predecessor, but still properly proportioned. The gaping front fascia tips off the GT-R's intended mission, as does the huge, adjustable rear wing. And the GT-R's round quad taillamps, when lit, cast the eerie glow of little jet afterburners. The black Supra (relieved of its rear wing) looks a bit dull in comparison. The Corvette looks unhappy, fitted with awkward fender flares in order to conform to Japanese fender-to-tire proportion regulations.

The GT-R's insides are from the Maxima school: dark gray with simple lines, austere and businesslike. Gauges let you monitor oil temperature, turbo boost, and torque to the front wheels. The monoform front seats, with just fore-and-aft and seatback-angle adjustments, provide terrific support. Four adults will fit in a GT-R comfortably. Try that in a 911.

Look at the Skyline's center console and interior floor, though, and you'll notice significant asymmetry right-to-left. This, combined with the engine-bay layout in which the six-cylinder is canted to the passenger side, reveals an obvious, depressing fact: it would take a cross-wired Star Trek replicator, if not an act of God, to make a left-hand-drive Skyline GT-R for the U.S.

Then again, there's always the customizing work of a Lugar Big Top, in the skillful hands of Motoko Yoshikawa. ●

Vehicle type: front-engine, four-wheel-drive, 4-passenger, 2-door sedan

Price as tested (Japan): $55,200 (base price: $54,600)

Options on test car: Superfine Hardcoat Paint, rear wiper, floormats

Major standard accessories: power steering, windows, and locks, A/C, tilt steering, rear defroster

Sound system: Nissan HH083 AM/FM-stereo radio/cassette, 4 speakers

ENGINE
Type ....twin-turbocharged and intercooled 6-in-line, iron block and aluminum head
Bore x stroke ....3.39 x 2.90 in, 86.0 x 73.7mm
Displacement ....157 cu in, 2569cc
Compression ratio 8.5:1
Engine-control system ....Nissan ECCS with port fuel injection
Emissions controls....................3-way catalytic converter, feedback fuel-air-ratio control, EGR
Turbocharger ....2 Garrett T3-T25
Waste gate ....integral
Maximum boost pressure......................................12.0 psi
Valve gear ....belt-driven double overhead cams, 4 valves per cylinder, solid lifters
Power (SAE net)............................276 bhp @ 6800 rpm
Torque (SAE net).............................271 lb-ft @ 4400 rpm
Redline...8000 rpm

DRIVETRAIN
Transmission..5-speed
Final-drive ratio....................4.11:1, electronic center and rear limited slip

Gear	Ratio	Mph/1000 rpm	Max. test speed
I	3.21	5.6	45 mph (8000 rpm)
II	1.93	9.3	74 mph (8000 rpm)
III	1.30	13.8	110 mph (8000 rpm)
IV	1.00	17.9	113 mph (6300 rpm)
V	0.75	23.9	113 mph (4750 rpm)

DIMENSIONS AND CAPACITIES
Wheelbase..107.1 in
Track, F/R...58.3/58.7 in
Length ....184.1 in

Width ....70.1 in
Height ....53.5 in
Ground clearance..5.3 in
Curb weight...3574 lb
Weight distribution, F/R 54.9/45.1%
Fuel capacity..17.2 gal
Oil capacity...5.4 qt
Water capacity..9.5 qt

CHASSIS/BODY
Type ....unit construction with a rubber-isolated rear subframe
Body material.........welded steel stampings with stamped aluminum front fenders and hood

INTERIOR
Front seats...bucket
Seat adjustments ....fore and aft, seatback angle
Restraint systems, front....................manual 3-point belts, driver airbag
rear ....manual 3-point belts
General comfort ....poor fair good **excellent**
Fore-and-aft support.....................poor fair good **excellent**
Lateral support ....poor fair good **excellent**

SUSPENSION
F: ....ind, unequal-length control arms, coil springs, anti-roll bar
R: ....ind, lower control arm with 2 lateral links per side, coil springs, anti-roll bar

STEERING
Type, F: ....rack-and-pinion, power-assisted
R: ....electronically controlled, hydraulically activated
Turns lock-to-lock...2.4
Turning circle curb-to-curb......................................37.4 ft

BRAKES
F: ....12.8 x 1.2-in vented disc
R: ....11.8 x 0.9-in vented disc
Power assist ....vacuum with anti-lock control

WHEELS AND TIRES
Wheel size ....9.0 x 17 in
Wheel type ....forged aluminum
Tires ....Bridgestone Expedia S-07, 245/45ZR-17
Test inflation pressures, F/R ....33/33 psi

CAR AND DRIVER TEST RESULTS

ACCELERATION
	Seconds
Zero to 30 mph	2.0
40 mph	2.7
50 mph	4.3
60 mph	5.3
70 mph	6.6
80 mph	9.1
90 mph	10.9
100 mph	12.9
110 mph	16.1
Street start, 5–60 mph	6.0
Top-gear passing time, 30–50 mph	11.8
50–70 mph	9.1
Standing ¼-mile	14.0 sec @ 104 mph
Top speed (governor limited)	113 mph

BRAKING
70–0 mph @ impending lockup ....159 ft

Fade ....**none** light moderate heavy

HANDLING
Roadholding, 300-ft-dia skidpad ....0.94 g
Understeer ....**minimal** moderate excessive

FUEL ECONOMY
Japanese city cycle...**19 mpg**
Steady 37 mph..34 mpg
C/D observed fuel economy ....**11 mpg**

INTERIOR SOUND LEVEL
Idle..47 dBA
Full-throttle acceleration ....81 dBA
70-mph cruising ....72 dBA
70-mph coasting ....71 dBA

Reach for
SKYLI

THE SOUND YOU CAN HEAR IS DISTANT ROLLING THUNDER. THE NISSAN SKYLINE, JAPAN'S GREATEST SUPERCAR, IS FINALLY HEADING FOR THE UK. THIS IS OUR TRIBUTE TO A PERFORMANCE CAR ICON

How hot would Sir like his Skyline? Taking centre stage is the standard Skyline GT-R R-spec with a mere 276bhp; on the right is the 370bhp Stage 1, and on the left Stage 2, with a serious 440bhp

the SKYLINE

Words: Richard Meaden. Pictures: Dominic Fraser

Skyline. It's an absurd name isn't it? What on earth does it mean? Sure, a word name is better than a number, like 200SX for instance, but it still seems somewhat odd that almost 30 years ago someone in a Nissan (or Datsun as it was then) creative meeting stood up and said, 'Right then. You know this new race-bred road car thingy the motorsport boys are building? I think we should call it "Skyline". Perfect, eh?'

Weird name or not, I bet you can't help feeling a slight flutter of excitement when you hear it mentioned. It's just one of those car names, like 'Integrale'

or 'Diablo', that has a strange effect on car fans. Few cars have such a cult following, fewer still prompt so many sage nods, knowing sucking of teeth and unconditional adoration from the cruelly discerning British performance car buying *cognoscenti*. The Skyline has got that intangible, crucial, never-to-be-underestimated thing called charisma. Respect, it would appear, is most definitely due.

Some great Japanese cars have been less fortunate in the past. ▷

REACH FOR THE SKYLINE

Skyline at dawn

Although we poor deprived Brits could be forgiven for thinking that Nissan's Skyline GT-R is a recent phenomenon, it does in fact date back to the last knockings of the 1960s.

Needing a car with racing potential, the Japanese manufacturing giant built the first Skyline GT-R in 1969. It enjoyed considerable competition success in domestic championships into the early 1970s. However, after creating an enviable image for the brand name, Nissan then proceeded to stick the moniker onto all manner of dismal, boxy saloons and coupés (see below).

Fortunately the company came to its senses in the late '80s, designing and building what many still regard as the definitive Skyline GT-R, the R32 (see 'Blue Thunder'). With pioneering use of twin ceramic turbos and intelligent four-wheel-drive, the R32 wiped the floor in top-level motorsport around the world, although sadly it was never officially sold in the UK.

When the latest R33 Skyline GT-R was launched, it took Nissan's flagship a stage further, with an even more effective all-wheel-drive transmission, a lap record at the Nürburgring and ever-growing cult status. Thankfully, this time it's coming to the UK.

▷ The Supra, RX-7 and Celica GT-Four have all bitten the dust despite being excellent cars in their own right. Even the brilliant NSX still suffers from a decidedly half-hearted following. No, if you want a Jap supercar with cast-iron cred, look no further than the Nissan Skyline GT-R.

In this respect Nissan's *ichiban* sports car is unique.

Of course, the big Skyline news of the moment is that, at last, Nissan has decided to import its greatest car to the one market that's been longing for it the most. The UK. Great news, even if the new R33 V-spec Skyline is only coming in very limited numbers (100 cars are due to be sold over the next two years from November 1). The Skyline has been big news with British car nuts for years, and this small but devoted group of people have played no small part in pressuring Nissan into doing the right thing and officially importing the Skyline. They've done it by buying cars from Japan and importing them on a purely personal basis, thereby proving there's demand for, and interest in, the cars.

Huge fans of the Skyline ourselves, we're bringing together three of the latest R33 Skylines in various states of tune, from a standard 276bhp to a whopping 440bhp, along with one of the most potent previous-generation Skylines in the country, an awesome 510bhp R32. We've figured all of them at Millbrook, driven them hard on our favourite roads, and dug up all the nuggets of Skyline folklore that make this formidable

This is a standard Skyline motor, good for 276bhp. Should this prove insufficient, you can more than double the output, easily. Nice thought

'In this car you feel untouchable, such is the level of grip, grunt and relentless acceleration...'

Blue thunder

All right, so this isn't a current Nissan Skyline, but to be perfectly honest we don't really care. For one thing it's got a flame-throwing 510bhp on tap, and for another it's got a racing clutch and six-speed, straight-cut gearbox to make full use of it.

In truth, the main reason we wanted its owner, Tim Milne, to bring his eyeball assaulting 'Calsonic blue' R32 Skyline along was to put some real 'no mercy'

figures to a highly tuned Skyline. All the cars in this feature are privately owned, and none of the R33 models had competition clutches, so we had to be unusually gentle. In Tim's car we could throw caution to the wind. 'Give it 7000rpm and drop the clutch,' said Tim. 'OK, if you insist,' said our man Barker. Bringing the revs up close to the redline, straight-six engine yowling deeply though the chimney-sized, de-

catted exhaust, JB prepared for take-off. Here, in his own words is what he experienced. 'JEeeeezzZ! Crack of gears, second – 0 to 30mph in 1.3secs (faster than a McLaren F1). Crack, third – 60mph in 3.697secs. Hold tight. Crack, fourth – 100mph in just 8.9secs. And so on, to 150mph in 27.2secs, by which time weight and aerodynamics have reined it in.' What he doesn't say is that this is one of the very fastest cars he's

ever figured. By the slightly flushed look on his face, JB has just fallen in love.

After driving it for the cornering shots, I can't say I blame him. It is quite simply amazing. In this car you feel untouchable, such is the amount of grip, grunt, relentless acceleration and incredibly friendly on-limit handling. In a 500bhp+ Porsche 911, cornering shots would be deeply scary; in this Skyline they are an absolute blast. Painting big black lines on the road has never been so much fun.

Tim got his 1991 R32 from a dealer in Japan, who had spent somewhere in the region of £20,000 on the engine, suspension and brakes. Forget Stage 1 or 2 tune, this is full-on 'Nutter' spec. Larger steel turbos for really big boost, hotter camshaft, oil cooler and larger intercooler, Ohlins dampers and springs, six-pot AP brake callipers and discs, adjustable boost control, twin-plate clutch, six-speed Quaife dog 'box and a Nismo bodykit make this the most extreme Skyline in the UK. Naturally, fast road driving and the odd track excursion are where this old warhorse really stretches its legs, but for the majority of the time this Skyline commutes across London.

With the introduction of the R33, prices of R32s are remarkably reasonable. If you fancy one, call Middlehurst Nissan, the UK's Skyline specialist, on 01744 26681. Expect to pay anywhere between £20,000-£30,000, depending on the state of tune.

The sky's the limit

As you've probably gathered by now, the Skyline's tuning potential is just about limitless. What you see pictured above is the ultimate Nissan Skyline: 980bhp worth of Japanese-tuned VeilSide Evolution R-1 Skyline GT-R R32 Combat, complete with six-speed HKS gearbox, twin oversize HKS turbos with steel rotors, 18in wheels, full carbon-look interior, and a complete wind tunnel-tested VeilSide wide-arch Combat bodykit, all finished off with a few coats of VeilSide Combat silver paint. Nice.

Laugh at the ridiculous name and excessive spec at your peril. The R-1 Combat holds the Japanese street car record for the standing quarter mile, a ripping 10.1secs with all four road-legal tyres smoking furiously. The McLaren F1 takes a tardy 11.1secs. Who's laughing now?

four-wheel-drive the greatest supercar Japan has ever produced.

Talking to David Yu, founder of the Skyline GT-R Register and complete Skyline nut, it's clear that buying a standard Skyline is merely the beginning of something very big. It's such an eminently tuneable car, so comfortable delivering and handling huge amounts of power that the standard car's 276bhp seems criminally conservative. Even Nissan acknowledges this fact, and although the UK-bound Skylines are leaving the factory with two-seven-six, there is the option of getting UK Skyline seller, Middlehurst Nissan, to pep them up to 350bhp without affecting the three-year parts and labour warranty. There's confidence for you.

As a result of this megalomania, finding a standard Skyline is tricky. Fortunately Nigel Wates was more than willing to bring his silver car along for us to try. This is his fourth Skyline but the first R33. He bought it in Tokyo while working out there on business, and decided to bring it back with him. It's an R-spec which means it hasn't got the super-sophisticated intelligent four-wheel- drive system of the V-spec, but it does have the same 276bhp as standard. Outwardly there's very little to tell it apart from the tuned cars – or indeed a

standard V-spec – but standard output or not it's a massively imposing car. The front fixes you a hard stare, jutting front chin spoiler and gaping cooling grilles adding that extra bit of menace. Flared wheelarches give it a pumped-up, powerfully muscled physique, and the tall, adjustable rear wing gives it a racing edge. It's clearly a descendant of the

smaller, less muscle-bound R32, the biggest styling cue being the traditional twin round tail-lights, but it's got a definite '90s look. Some feel it's a bit plain and lacking in flamboyance. Drive it and you soon understand that the no-frills styling matches the Skyline's no-nonsense road manners.

Everything about the Skyline inspires

confidence and builds your expectations. First impressions come thick and fast. The driving position is excellent and easy to perfect, the pedals require positive pressure, the steering is devoid of wooliness (although it is ever-so-slightly numb), the ride has a Porsche RS quality to its firmness, the gearshift rewards fast, precise use and the drivetrain feels taut, solid and strong. Above all, you get the feeling that the Skyline is built with one job in mind. Going very quickly indeed.

Even when you're not really trying, speed builds effortlessly. Just stroking up through the gears, never using more than 5000rpm and barely squeezing the throttle more than halfway, the Skyline is soon up to license-losing velocity. Already it's clear the only time you have to try is when you want to drive slowly. That's not to say the Skyline is a peaky, on/off sort of car. Flexibility is a strong point of the smooth 2.6-litre straight-six motor, with lusty reserves of power and torque supplied via two low-inertia ceramic turbos.

The same is true of Joss Ellis's black R33, even when taken to 370bhp Stage 1 tune. All this entails is a chip change and an outlay of around £500 – pretty simple stuff that reaps huge rewards. There's much more grunt everywhere, which in turn makes better use of the chassis and sharpens the whole feel of the car. In many respects this is the ideal state of tune, as you get a bigger slug of power without any great increase in throttle response, it costs relatively little and components like the clutch and gearbox aren't overly stressed. If, as David says,

Sky Sports

The Nurbürgring is where a car's reputation is made or smashed into splinters. Many manufacturers claim to have developed their high-performance cars on the Nordschleif's formidable 14 miles and 70-plus corners (the BMW M5 even had a Nurbürgring handling pack), but only one can claim to build the production car lap record holder. Although it's a strictly unofficial benchmark, being the quickest around the toughest race track in the world is a much coveted claim to fame. Drive the circuit yourself and you'll soon come to realise why the Skyline R33's sub-8 minute lap in the hands of Dirk Schoysman is held in such reverence.

REACH FOR THE SKYLINE

you want yet more power, it comes at a price. For around £2000, power can be lifted to 440bhp with the fitment of a remapped chip and steel turbos for bigger boost pressure. The downside is a loss of response, the heavier steel turbo internals taking longer to spool up to speed, but boy, when they're spinning the Stage 2

Skyline has serious thrust, as Paul Pheysey's car demonstrated.

I should tell you that in deference to the clutches of all these cars, we avoided full-blooded Millbrook launches. Turbocharged four-wheel-drive cars are notoriously difficult when it comes to standing starts, and often the only way to

get them off the line without bogging down is to dial-in a huge amount of revs and sidestep the clutch. If it works you get a great 0-60mph time; if it doesn't you get a fried clutch. Instead we employed a highly restrained technique, feeding the clutch in as you would when accelerating briskly away from a set of traffic lights. With this in mind, a 0-60mph time in the low fives, as Joss Ellis's car turned in, is rather more impressive than you first think, as is the 0-100mph time of 12.6secs.

PERFORMANCE

	276bhp R33	370bhp R33	440bhp R33	510bhp R32
Max speed (mph)*limited	112*	n/a	n/a	n/a
Through the gears (secs)				
0-30mph	2.9	2.0	2.9	1.5
0-40mph	3.8	2.9	3.8	2.1
0-50mph	5.0	4.0	5.0	2.9
0-60mph	**6.3**	**5.2**	**6.2**	**3.7**
0-70mph	7.7	6.55	7.7	4.7
0-80mph	9.64	8.41	9.64	6.0
0-90mph	11.66	10.4	11.7	7.2
0-100mph	**14.3**	**12.6**	**14.0**	**8.2**
0-110mph	17.23	15.6	17.2	10.7
Standing ¼mile (secs/mph)	14.7/102	13.7/104	14.1/106	12.0/113
TED* (secs/ft)	5.0/460	4.7/510	4.9/450	4.3/415

*(Time Exposed to Danger) Time and distance required to overtake an articulated lorry travelling at a constant 45mph.

3rd/4th gear acceleration (secs)				
20-40mph	5.2/7.7	6.0/8.4	5.4/7.6	4.3/6.0
30-50mph	**4.2/6.6**	**4.9/7.2**	**4.3/6.5**	**3.5/5.3**
40-60mph	3.5/5.6	3.9/6.2	3.4/5.5	2.7/4.3
50-70mph	3.3/4.8	3.2/5.2	3.3/4.7	2.1/3.4
60-80mph	3.5/4.4	3.0/4.3	3.3/4.2	2.1/2.8
70-90mph	3.7/4.7	3.3/4.9	3.5/4.4	3.1/2.7
80-100mph	4.3/5.1	3.7/4.2	4.0/4.8	---/2.7
90-110mph	---/5.5	---/4.6	---/5.3	---/2.9

5th/6th gear acceleration (secs)				
20-40mph	---/---	---/---	---/---	8.7/---
30-50mph	11.4/---	12.2/---	11.5/---	8.0/10.7
40-60mph	10.4/---	11.3/---	10.2/---	7.3/10.2
50-70mph	**9.3/---**	**10.3/---**	**9.2/---**	**6.4/9.5**
60-80mph	8.2/---	9.4/---	8.3/---	5.3/8.6
70-90mph	7.7/---	6.1/---	7.4/---	4.4/7.3
80-100mph	7.6/---	7.2/---	7.1/---	3.8/6.5

Sky at night

To join Mid Night, Japan's most notorious and hardest of hardcore street racing clubs, you could do a lot worse than buy a Skyline. Membership requirements are tough, and there are only 30 Mid Nighters, despite the club's 12-year history. All of these shady characters have hugely modified cars capable of more than 175mph, and more importantly the inclination and sheer brain-out ability to drive them flat-out on the Bayshore expressway between Tokyo and Yokohama.

There's all manner of exotica, from massively modified RX-7s, Supras and Porsche 911s to the odd Ferrari, but to really cut it at a Mid Night meet you need a Skyline. Not only will you be thankful for the GT-R's four-wheel-drive traction and forgiving handling, but you'll also have something in common with Mid Night's club manager, who runs a 650bhp, 200mph R32 Skyline. It sure beats joining the Caravan Club.

SPECIFICATION

	Nissan Skyline GT-R V-spec
Engine	In-line six, twin-turbo
Location	Front, longitudinal
Displacement	2568cc
Bore x stroke	86mm x 73.7mm
Compression ratio	10.4 to one
Cylinder block	Cast-iron
Cylinder head	Aluminium alloy, dohc, 24v
Max power	276bhp @ 6800rpm
Max torque	271lb ft @ 4400rpm
Transmission	Five-speed manual, intelligent four-wheel-drive
Front suspension	Independent, multi-link, coil springs, anti-roll bar
Rear suspension	Independent, multi-link, coil springs, anti-roll bar
Steering	Super HICAS 4WS, pas
Brakes	Brembo vented discs, 4-pot front, 2-pot rear, anti-lock
Wheels	9J x 17in, cast alloy
Tyres	245/45 ZR17 Bridgestone
Weight (kerb/test)	3396/3725lb
Power-to-weight (test)	166bhp per ton
Basic price	£50,000 (estimated)
Airbag driver/pass	standard
Air conditioning	standard
Alarm immobiliser	standard
Anti-lock brakes	standard
Adj steering column	standard
Sunroof	n/a
Price	£50,000 (estimated)
Insurance group	20

Paul Pheysey was disappointed with the times his car put in, and after having his car checked by Middlehurst's it was found to be running at 0.8 bar boost pressure rather than the expected 1.2 bar, which means it was probably 100bhp down. For a true demonstration of what a proper dropped-clutch start in a 510bhp Skyline will produce, read 'Blue Thunder' on page 79.

Acceleration is only half the Skyline story. The chassis is equally impressive, both for its phenomenal technology and its ability to thrill. Normally the combination of four-wheel-drive and more sensors than a deep space probe makes for deadly dull motoring. Just look at the Mitsubishi 3000GT. In the Skyline it is sensational. In ordinary use, power is sent to the rear wheels. If the intelligent 4wd system detects any loss of traction, power is fed to the front as well.

Where it gets really clever is that it can sense loss of grip at any wheel and act on it independently, splitting the power between back, front and individual wheels. Sounds like a recipe for zero fun, but Nissans's chassis men are better than that. Fun is part of the equation, and although you'd be hard-pushed to get power oversteer out of a standard V-spec R33 on the road, give the chassis more power than it knows what to do with and you can drift around to your heart's content. It is quite simply the most incredibly exploitable, enjoyable and throttle adjustable all-whee-drive chassis ever made.

The Skyline GT-R deserves the hero worship. Stupendous in standard trim, startlingly potent when tuned, it's already one of the most keenly awaited cars of 1997. Unique in character, style and the way it delivers its performance, it towers above its opposition. Perhaps it's not such a stupid name afer all. ●

Many thanks to David Yu, Nigel Wates, Paul Pheysey, Joss Ellis and Tim Milne from the Skyline GT-R Register (for more details on the Register call David Yu on 0181 723 8127). If you'd like to see the largest gathering of UK Skylines in action, get along to the Japanese Supercar Club track day at Cadwell Park on Saturday August 16. If you want to take part, contact Alan Davis on 01778 570136.

Nissan SKYLINE

MODEL TESTED GTR V-spec **LIST PRICE** £50,000
TOP SPEED 155mph (limited) **30-70MPH** 4.8sec
0-60MPH 5.0sec **60-0MPH** 2.9sec **MPG** 19.6
FOR Blistering performance, fine handling, stability, brakes
AGAINST Fuel tank's too small, noisy high-speed ride

The Skyline GTR is the car we've been waiting for Nissan GB to deliver for years. Apart from being a technical tour de force thanks to items like four-wheel drive and four-wheel steering, it is also one of the most underrated driver's cars we have ever encountered.

Developed largely at the gruelling Nürburgring in Germany by a crack team of enthusiasts who know exactly what it is that distinguishes a fast car from a great one, the Skyline has already proved itself on more than one occasion within these pages. So the news that it will be on sale officially from next month at a list price of £50,000, supported by a proper three-year Nissan warranty, is cause for celebration.

There will be just one version available, the V-spec, which in Skyline speak means sports suspension, 277bhp and 17in wheels and tyres. And because of import restrictions, only 100 will be available over the next five years. Exclusivity, therefore, will be guaranteed for the Skyline in the UK.

TOM SALT

DESIGN & ENGINEERING

The GTR version of this originally two and four-door rear-drive saloon was built to win the All Japan Touring Car Championship. This dictates the 2.6-litre engine size. When Nissan re-entered the AJTCC, Sierra Cosworths were dominant. To be competitive, a minimum of 600bhp was needed for the race version. And because wheel rim widths were restricted to 10in, the decision to go four-wheel drive was an obvious one.

What Nissan calls ATTESA-ETS PRO is a part-time four-wheel drive system that puts handling first, directing power to the rear wheels until conditions demand otherwise. Sensors of individual wheel speed, longitudinal and lateral acceleration, throttle opening and brake light activation give the electronic control unit enough indication of wheelspin,

stability and driver intention. The ECU acts on two electro-hydraulic wet-plate clutches, one working as a rear locking differential, the other as part of the centre differential. That way, up to half the engine's torque can be transferred via a chain transfer drive to the front, for stability out of a corner.

Super-HICAS four-wheel steering involves sensors of steering rate, steering rate acceleration and yaw rate (how fast the vehicle actually turns in response to driver input). In effect, the electronics can compare steering input and output – what the car actually does. The rear-wheel steer is entirely electronically controlled, via a small electric steering rack. In the event of an electric failure, a hefty spring returns the rear wheels to the straight ahead. In a corner, the rear wheels initially steer in the opposite direction to the front wheels (oversteer), to sharpen initial steering response; then on sensing that the car has responded they steer the same way as the fronts (understeer), which sharpens the steering by taking up some rear tyre slip angle.

Each set of three cylinders in the iron-block 24-valve in-line six has its own Garrett T3/T25 intercooled turbocharger, blowing at up to 12psi.

Racing-inspired technology is put to good use here ★ ★ ★ ★

PERFORMANCE/BRAKES

Performance is laggy but potent

There is a school of thought that reckons the standard Skyline, with a mere 277bhp and 271lb ft, is nowhere near fast enough. The 2568cc twin-turbo straight six engine is apparently game for tuning to well beyond 500bhp and can be made to produce 360bhp with very little work other than the fitment of a new chip. But as this affects the warranty and exacerbates the already laggy throttle response, you'll need to be seriously committed to have this work carried out, especially since the standard car is not exactly what many people would call slow.

From a standstill, 60mph comes up in 5.0sec dead thanks to the fabulous four-wheel drive traction off the line (0-30mph in 1.9sec). To 100mph it requires just 13.0sec. And between these two markers it gets from 30-70mph in 4.7sec, making it broadly as quick as a six-speed Honda NSX on acceleration, if not quite on top speed, where the Skyline is limited to 155mph.

For a Japanese car that encorporates so much technology, the Skyline has an unusual amount of what is best described as character. The straight six emits a wonderfully fruity bark at low to medium revs, while at high revs there is a variety of intriguing noises that underscore the mechanical operations, including some outrageous whistles from the turbos and wastegates.

There is only one real snag to the performance, and that's the turbo lag. Open the throttle in any gear below 3300rpm and you need to wait whole seconds for the blowers to force air back through the engine. In fifth gear (24.8mph per 1000rpm) the wait can seem like forever, as the 10.2sec 50-70mph time all too clearly illustrates.

The only way to drive around this is to drop one or even two ratios in the five-speed gearbox and put the engine back in the band where it delivers its biggest punch, between 5000 and 7500rpm. There is little point in going higher because in standard tune the straight six goes off the boil between here and the 8000rpm red line.

Not that it is much of a hardship driving the Skyline like this. The gearchange is very crisp and precise, while the clutch is as easy on the calf muscles as any Nissan's.

The brakes are also strong and powerful, hauling the 1601kg Skyline to a rest with good feel and no fade.

Huge performance – and lag – from characterful engine ★ ★ ★ ★

HANDLING & RIDE

Given the amount of technology that's bubbling away beneath the Skyline GTR's skin, it might be asking too much for it to also be one of the great communicators. Not so. By painstaking development of the chassis around the Nürburgring, Nissan has somehow managed to create a car that will not only astound drivers with its outrageous objective handling capabilities but also one that is bursting with feel and feedback.

Take the steering. Although there can be drive to the front to theoretically corrupt the flow of information, not to mention an extra electronic steering rack at the rear, the relationship between tarmac, wheel rim and driver's fingers is as intimate and involving as it is in any Porsche currently on sale.

Then there's the unique combination of grip, body control, handling stability and plain old seat-of-the-pants communication. By programming the front drive to disengage completely in normal driving and to administer no more than 50 per cent of the drive to the front wheels even in extreme situations, Nissan has succeeded in getting the Skyline to feel and behave like a very well-sorted rear-wheel-drive car, rather than a four-wheel-drive one, even to the point where it can be made to deliver lurid power slides where conditions permit – something that no other four-wheel-drive

road car has been capable of in our experience.

On the other hand, traction and wet-weather grip are as good as, if not better than they are in the best conventional four-wheel-drive cars. Indeed, Nissan claims that the Skyline fails to show its true colours until driven quickly in the pouring rain over an impossible road. From our experience of it in the damp over some challenging Welsh mountain passes, we're inclined to agree.

And the downsides? Unusually, we can think of no

Huge stability *and* great feel

significant handling criticisms. The Skyline GTR is quite simply one of the all-time great ground coverers, blending feel and ability in a rare and delicious cocktail. The only slight drawback is the ride. At all times the suspension is hard, but just occasionally it becomes crashy, too. The big Bridgestone tyres sometimes thump into deep ruts and the chassis never quite recovers. Otherwise it rides pretty smoothly considering how tightly controlled it is.

Unparalleled A-to-B ability coupled with great feel ★ ★ ★ ★ ★

Skyline is the only four-wheel-drive road car in which this sort of thing is possible in our experience

PERFORMANCE AND SPECIFICATIONS

ENGINE

Layout 6 cyls in line, 2568cc
Max power 277bhp at 6800rpm
Max torque 271lb ft at 4400rpm
Specific output 108bhp per litre
Power to weight 173bhp per tonne
Torque to weight 169lb ft per tonne
Installation front, longitudinal, four-wheel drive
Construction alloy head, iron block
Bore/stroke 86.0/73.7mm
Valve gear 4 valves per cyl, dohc
Compression ratio 8.5:1
Ignition and fuel Sequential injection, twin Garrett T25 turbochargers

GEARBOX

Type 5-speed manual
Ratios/mph per 1000rpm
1st 3.21/5.8 **2nd** 1.92/9.8
3rd 1.30/14.3 **4th** 1.00/18.6
5th 0.75/24.8
Final drive ratio 4.11:1

MAXIMUM SPEEDS

5th 155mph/6250rpm **4th** 149/8000
3rd 114/8000 **2nd** 78/8000
1st 46/8000

ACCELERATION FROM REST

True mph	sec	speedo mph
30	1.9	31
40	2.7	41
50	3.8	51
60	5.0	61
70	6.6	72
80	8.5	82
90	10.5	92
100	13.0	103
110	16.8	113
120	20.0	123
130	24.1	134

Standing qtr mile 13.7sec/102mph
Standing kilo 24.7sec/131mph
30-70 in gears 4.7sec

ACCELERATION IN GEARS

mph	5th	4th	3rd	2nd
10-30	–	–	6.7	4.1
20-40	13.8	8.1	5.6	3.0
30-50	12.4	6.9	4.4	2.3
40-60	11.6	5.7	3.5	2.3
50-70	10.2	4.7	3.3	2.6
60-80	8.5	4.4	3.5	–
70-90	7.8	5.0	3.7	–
80-100	7.9	5.2	4.1	–
90-110	9.6	5.3	–	–
100-120	11.7	6.5	–	–
110-130	13.9	8.0	–	–

STEERING

Type Rack and pinion, power assisted, speed sensitive, Super-HICAS four-wheel steer
Turns lock to lock 2.8

CONTROLS IN DETAIL

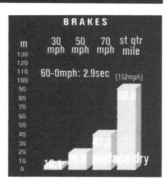

1 Rev counter redlined at 8000rpm; more applicable after the engine has been chipped (which most owners will do) 2 Stereo folds away electrically to leave a blank in the dash 3 Five-speed 'box feels very tough, though not unnecessarily heavy 4 Torque gauge tells how much drive is being transmitted to the front axle; it's dormant for most of the time 5 Seats are terrific; seriously supportive 6 Chunky Momo wheel looks and feels great

SUSPENSION

Front multi-link, coil springs, anti-roll bar
Rear multi-link, coil springs, anti-roll bar

WHEELS AND TYRES

Wheel size 9Jx17in
Made of cast alloy **Tyres** 245/45 ZR17 Bridgestone S-02
Spare space saver

BRAKES

Front 324mm ventilated discs
Rear 300mm ventilated discs
Anti-lock standard

BRAKES

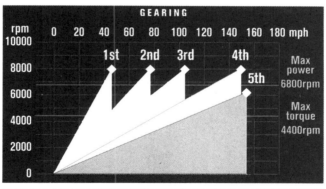

60-0mph: 2.9sec

GEARING

FUEL CONSUMPTION

TEST RESULTS

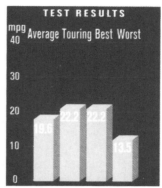

mpg — Average 19.6, Touring 22.2, Best 22.2, Worst 13.5

GOVERNMENT CLAIMS

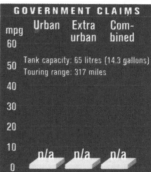

Urban n/a, Extra urban n/a, Combined n/a
Tank capacity: 65 litres (14.3 gallons)
Touring range: 317 miles

NOISE

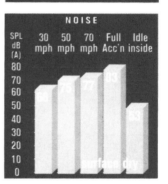

LAYOUT

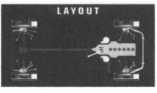

AUTOCAR road tests are conducted using BP Unleaded or BP Diesel Plus with additives to help keep engines cleaner

Body 2dr coupe **Cd** 0.35 **Front/rear tracks** 1480/1490mm **Turning circle** 11.4m **Min/max front leg room** 910/1080mm **Min/max rear leg room** 610/790mm **Min/max front head room** 880/940mm **Rear head room** 850mm **Interior width front/rear** 1420/1390mm **Boot length/width/height** 590/1320/490mm **VDA boot volume** n/a **Kerb weight** 1601kg **Distribution f/r** n/a **Max payload** 299kg

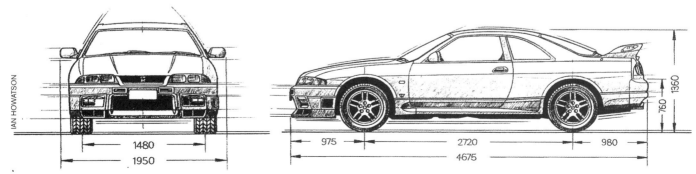

IAN HOWATSON

1480 / 1950

975 / 2720 / 980 / 4675 / 1360 / 760

Cabin is purposeful rather than beautiful. Seats offer terrific support and driving position is superb, but dash is pretty plain

COMFORT, EQUIPMENT & SAFETY

There are few frills to the Skyline's cabin. From the moment you climb aboard it becomes clear that the interior has been designed with the committed driver in mind, which is why you'll find a pair of fabulously supportive front seats, big, clear instruments and near-perfect location of all the controls, but little in the way of visual or tactile titillation.

The seats are covered in a grippy suede-like material, not leather, while the dashboard is finished in a black plastic that looks and feels no better qualitatively than that of a humble Primera's. It's not ugly, but neither is it what you'd describe as gorgeous.

Space in the rear is unique among 150mph-plus super-coupes. There is as much leg room in the rear as there is in a Primera, while head room is compromised only for passengers over 6ft tall. And the boot is a reasonable size, despite the CD autochanger and adjustable rear anti-roll bar

Decent boot, despite CD changer

that nibble into luggage room.

There are few options, but only because Nissan GB has thought intelligently about the standard specification. Climate control, multi-disc CD changer and a full anti-theft system are included in the basic specification, as is a height-adjustable driver's seat and tilt-adjustable wheel. There is also an ingenious stereo front that folds away electrically to leave a blank panel on the dash when the car's not in use.

It is difficult to imagine a car with markedly greater active safety than the GTR. As well as four-wheel drive, anti-lock brakes and stability-aiding four-wheel steer, there are twin airbags and pre-tensioners on the front seatbelts (but not those in the rear).

ECONOMY

Judging from the speed with which the needle plummets on the fuel gauge during hard driving, one might expect the consumption to be only just this side of horrendous. But in the event, this is mostly the result of a woefully small 65-litre (14.4-gallon) fuel tank. Actual economy is not at all bad considering the ferocity of the performance: 19.6mpg overall, rising to 22.2mpg over our touring route. Even so, having to pull in and find a garage that sells 98-octane unleaded every 250-280 miles is one of the Skyline's most irritating foibles.

Blown six needs 98-octane unleaded

Functional, not beautiful, but roomy and well equipped ★★★★

Acceptable economy spoiled by small fuel tank, poor range ★★★

Skyline is unique among 150mph super-coupes in offering fine rear space

MARKET & FINANCE

The Skyline GTR may have "nutter" written all over it, but in truth it's hard to think of a more sensible supercar.

It shouldn't lose too much money, firstly because it's so desirable and secondly because just 100 will be sold in the UK over the next five years. Still, that price looks a little high. Word is that used Skylines will fetch premiums to begin with, but we're more inclined to think prices of around £45,000 are more likely over the next year or so, certainly once the initial excitement has died away a bit.

Then there are the people who sell and service the car: Andy Middlehurst Nissan of St Helens. They've sold more Skylines than anyone else in the country. Andy Middlehurst himself won the National Saloon Car Championship in 1995 and last year in a Skyline. The point is, the people who prepare his car service all Skylines, too, so they know exactly what they're doing. Services are every 6000 and 12,000 miles. The 12,000 costs roughly £400 and AM collects and returns your car for free.

The warranty is Nissan's standard three-year/60,000-mile deal. However, uprate the engine's power output and, according to Middlehurst, you'll seriously risk invalidating cover on any components damaged as a result.

It's difficult to be precise about insurance at this early stage, but broker Bennets Elite has just quoted a 47-year-old company director £604 fully comprehensive for insuring a 1995 GTR worth £38,000.

> **Great after-sale support and residual values, but pricey ★ ★ ★ ★**

Instruments are big and purposeful

WHAT IT COSTS

On-the-road price	£50,000
Total as tested	£50,000
Cost per mile	n/a

EQUIPMENT
(bold = options fitted to test car)

Automatic transmission	–
Remote central locking	●
Airbag driver/pass	●/●
Anti-lock brakes	●
Traction control	●
Alloy wheels	●
Alarm/immobiliser	●/●
RDS stereo/CD player	●/●
Steering column adjustment	●
Leather interior	–
Adjustable anti-roll bar	●
Cruise control	–
Air conditioning	●
● standard – not available	
Insurance group	**20**

WARRANTY
Three years/60,000 miles, Nissan Assist recovery

SERVICING
Major 12,000 miles, £351.00
Interim 6000 miles, £140.00

PART PRICES

Oil filter	£7.00
Air filter	£12.00
Brake pads f/r	£280.00
Set of sparkplugs (8)	£72.00
Exhaust (excluding cat)	£1200
Door mirror glass	£130
Tyre (each typical)	£255.00
Windscreen	£450.00
Headlamp unit	£202.00
Front wing	£177.00
Rear bumper	£390.00

THE AUTOCAR VERDICT

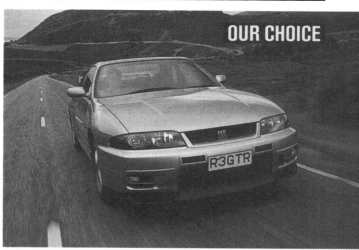

OUR CHOICE

Skyline is a blinding driver's car and is almost uncatchable across country

HOW THE RIVALS COMPARE

MAKE/MODEL	LIST PRICE	MPH/0-60	TEST DATE
Porsche Carrera	**£61,544**	**155/6.0sec**	**1.10.97**
On sale soon, new 911 is very fast and very good			★ ★ ★ ★
BMW Alpina B10	**£63,500**	**167/5.7sec**	**18.6.97**
An M5 in all but name. Hugely talented – at a hefty price			★ ★ ★ ★
Honda NSX	**£58,795**	**168/5.9sec**	**23.7.97**
An impressive supercar, but not legendary in this company			★ ★ ★ ★

The Skyline may have been a long time coming but, as you'll probably have guessed by now, it was well worth the wait. It is, quite simply, one of the finest driver's cars on sale today – the perfect antithesis of that other Japanese super-coupe with four-wheel drive and a twin-turbo engine, the disappointingly cumbersome Mitsubishi 3000 GT.

What distinguishes the Skyline from most other ultra-quick transport is that it successfully blends a huge amount of technological achievement with an even bigger level of tactile communication. And in doing so it ends up offering the best of both worlds on the road: titanic speed and peerless all-weather stability mated to exquisite feel and supreme driver involvement.

This makes it unique in our book, even beside the once inimitable Honda NSX. That car might have a better engine than the Skyline's explosive but laggy turbocharged six, but it has neither the steering delicacy nor the sheer cross-country pace of the Nissan – and it costs a not inconsiderable £20,000 more these days. Indeed, even the new £65,000 Porsche 911 would have difficulty matching it over uneven ground – on a communicative level, as well on straight speed.

The faults it carries are few and far between. Whether you love or loathe the looks, no one could argue that the Skyline lacks purpose visually, inside or out. It could use a bigger fuel tank, too. Having to fill up three times to get to Scotland is an irritation that the designers could surely have eradicated fairly easily, considering the overall size of the car. After that you're nit picking to find more serious problems.

The only real snag we can foresee will be the import restrictions that will limit the number of examples on our roads to just 100. We don't imagine the job of the Skyline salesman being all that tough to do, for example. Even at £50k it seems like good value.

If only there were more cars like this one.

> ### TEST NOTES
>
> The torque gauge on the centre console has to be the craziest gauge on any road car. It tells you how much drive is being apportioned to the front wheels at any given time, but it only works when the rear wheels start to slip. You don't tend to look at the gauges when you're drifting deftly through your favourite A-road bend.
>
> The next time you see a Skyline on the road, check to see how much wing the owner is running. By undoing a few allen bolts you can change the angle of the wing dramatically, but whether this affects rear-end stability on the way down to Tesco's is another matter. Having said that, it does alter the drag coefficient from 0.35 to 0.39...

Climate control air conditioning is standard; stereo hides away at a touch

The best Japanese super-coupe ever ★ ★ ★ ★ ★

HARD ROCK

Its coachwork may be made of glassfibre, but the **Lotus Esprit V8 GT** follows the spirit of the traditional **heavy**

widest, lowest body. The **Nissan Skyline GTR**, however, relies on the latest **computer** wizardry to achieve the

You've got money to spend – serious money – and you want the ultimate in sheer driving pleasure. You turn to the *Top Gear* blue pages and find two cars right on the button of your 50 grand budget. Two cars as different as they could possibly be – yet two cars that would precisely fit your bill.

Meet, in the left hand corner, the Lotus Esprit V8 GT, latest version of the slinky mid-engined supercar with an (albeit distant now) race-proved heritage and, in the right, the Nissan Skyline GTR, a bit of hi-tech wizardry about as pretty as a mouse-nibbled piece of cheese but with more letters after its name than a university of professors. Which, then, to pick?

The Lotus may be the company's newest model but it's virtually the

NEW WAVE

Photography: Simon Childs

metal performance car – just throw a twin-turbocharged V8 into the **middle** of the chassis and clothe it with the **same** effect – a huge great **grin** on the driver's face. So how does the **old rocker** compare to the **techno kid**?

same as the existing Esprit V8. Probably only the anorak will spot the GT's missing rear wing and a tell-tale V8 GT sticker in the rear quarterlights.

This Esprit's mechanical specs haven't changed much either – same mid-mounted 3.5-litre twin-turbo V8 with identical peak horsepower and torque figures at the same rpm. But the removal of the wing means the V8 GT has to be electronically limited to 170mph, compared to the V8's top speed of 175mph. Along with the absent wing, a stereo, leather upholstery, air conditioning and some soundproofing materials have been ditched as well, giving a modest 40kg reduction in weight and a massive £10,000 drop in price from the V8.

Compared to the traditionalist

Esprit, the Skyline is a radical technological tour de force with its computer-controlled four-wheel-drive and four-wheel steering. However, it does bow to convention in the fact that its body is made of metal not plastic and its twin-turbocharged, six-cylinder 276bhp motor sits at the front. Inside, it's more sensible saloon, rather than leery supercar, with four seats and a distinctly non-horizontal driving position. Quite the opposite to the Esprit.

To pit the trad beast against the techno pretender, we decided to treat them to a thrash round the testing roads of south-west Wales. The two cars met up for the first time at the first services west of the new Severn Bridge, with both drivers having already been reminded of these cars' phenomenal on-the-road performance.

Both being turbocharged, they each need a second or so to fully respond to a sudden application of right boot, but 'lag' wouldn't be a fair description. Both pull strongly from little above idle and gather momentum very rapidly once their needles hit the mid-range, but from around 2,500rpm on full throttle the V8 GT's enthusiasm for forward motion borders on the absurd.

Although the GT's peak power figures are the same as the Esprit V8's, it is burdened with less of the emissions control gubbins necessary for some overseas markets. So Lotus engineers have been able to flatten the GT's torque curve, giving it even more muscle where it's needed most.

Make no mistake, this car's quick. Not quite as outrageously rapid as a Cerbera or Diablo, but in the same ballpark as a 550 Maranello, taking the same 10.8 seconds to hit 100mph from rest and, at 18.7secs, a paltry two tenths longer to reach 130mph. We could argue till the cows come home about where to draw the line between 'supercar' and 'normalcar', but the V8 GT's most certainly one of the former.

Not that the big Nissan's a slouch. Dump the clutch at 7,000rpm, light up all four tyres and it'll hit the national limit in under seven seconds. A Lotus GT driver would need an awful lot of clear road ahead to safely overtake a GTR in a hurry – much more than you'll find within these shores.

Although the latest Esprit V8s have been fitted with a new five-speed Renault selector mechanism, the Lotus's gearchange is neither as swift nor as fluid as the Skyline's, whose shift feels as user-friendly as a

The Esprit V8 GT is the Led Zeppelin of supercars. The shape has lasted even longer than a John Bonham drum solo, and the whole concept has its roots as far back as Jimmy Page's blues riffs. Put your foot down and its brutal performance will get your head banging

Primera's. There's also a knack to engaging reverse on the Lotus, but perhaps the Esprit's biggest downfall is its clutch take-up from standstill.

The latest Esprit V8s have, I quote: 'A new, specially developed AP Racing twin-plate, pull-actuated, low-inertia clutch and actuation mechanism together with a redesigned bell housing' which, also according to Lotus: 'notably enhances driveability'. Setting off swiftly isn't a problem and, curious-

ly, neither is creeping back in reverse, but get stuck in a slow-moving, stop-start traffic jam and taking a long bath in hot petrol starts to seem more preferable, for it either wants to stall (which it does without qualm) or it revs like a BSM Metro on the first day of a beginner's course.

Though it's heavy and bites late and hard, this probably isn't entirely the new clutch's fault, because the throttle is over-sensitive and difficult to con-

trol. Even when you do get the balance about right (with practice, about a one-in-ten chance) the rear wheels judder and the whole car follows suit. Sorry Lotus, the Esprit's hardly new but more work is still needed here.

In contrast, the Skyline is incredibly easy to get along with in day-to-day driving. Although the interior wouldn't win any prizes for aesthetics, its contoured front seats hug the whole torso and all the controls are precisely where

66

Nissan's Skyline GTR is more of a Gary Numan, although a lot more exciting. It uses all the latest computer-controlled electronic devices with strange acronymic names like ATTESA E-TS PRO, and can be programmed to play 'Are Friends Electric' through its exhaust pipe

handshake. But no, of these two it's the Skyline that jiggles your organs about the most. At higher speeds the Nissan's suspension settles down and delivers the goods but get stuck behind a lorry on a B-road and your sunglasses will soon slide off the tip of your nose.

Again, the Esprit's ride improves with speed. At lower speeds we'd hardly describe it as luxurious but it's noticeably comfier than the Nissan's and considerably more supple than a mid-engined supercar has any right to be.

Where it's harder to pass judgement is on how they handle, as although they have quite different on-the-limit characteristics, both are exceptionally adept and fun. On an empty, twisting public road they're so brutally quick and capable that if you messed up on the outer edge of the envelope you'd probably wind up either in hospital, prison, or both.

In common with a handful of other super-quick road vehicles, two wheeled and four, the Skyline and Esprit's limits are really for track use only. Sure, you can force the Lotus into a comical slow understeer on a mini roundabout, and exiting a 90-degree junction you can safely step the rear out in either, but that's not what these cars were built for. The Esprit is, of course, lighter and doesn't carry anything like as much weight at the front so it's that bit more chuckable, but both turn in sharply, steer faithfully and grip, at least in the dry, with real vengeance.

So, having pressed our luck just a little beyond prudence, we dropped by the Pembrey circuit in Carmarthenshire for a spot of precision high-performance driving – or lairy skidding about, if you prefer.

We were expecting the V8 GT to be a bit of a handful on the track but, with a modicum of practice and respect, it can be comfortably steered on the throttle with the tyres drifting nicely. At precisely the moment the Lotus's Michelins squealed they simultaneously lost grip, at least on Pembrey's surface, so apart from the sensitive feedback through the steering there was also a clearly audible warning when the car broke loose. And when that happened there was thankfully still a workable window of control before you set off backwards onto the grass with the ABS working overtime.

The Skyline, as you perhaps already know, has banks of computers controlling the car's handling. Something called ATTESA E-TS PRO 'monitors

you want them. Rear headroom isn't generous but the back seats will carry adult passengers and there's standard aircon, airbags and a motor-driven 'self-camouflaging' Kenwood stereo control unit and mock Kevlar CD stacker in the boot to impress all but the most die-hard technophobes.

Lying down inside the race-car-like Lotus, things are just a bit cramped. With its removable roof panel in situ, there's headroom but it'll be borderline

if you're much over six foot. Though good, our test car's leather racing seat option (£595) isn't quite as comfy as the Nissan's, and being one-piece there's no backrest adjustment, which for taller drivers makes the wheel seem a little low while the rim partially obscures instrumentation.

The optional speakers mounted just beneath the windscreen look like an amateur afterthought and the lock on our glovebox fell to bits, but for the

most part the Esprit GT's cockpit is a pleasant place to be. Rear visibility is hardly panoramic but the interior trim, wheel, dash, alloy gear knob, colour-matched centre console and chromed gearstick gaiter rim are in keeping with the cost and nature of this car.

Both these cars roll on seriously low-profile rubber and, taking note of the Lotus's snake's-belly ride height, you could be forgiven for thinking that its ride is firmer than a Terminator's and controls the power delivery and braking force independently to all four wheels to allow each wheel to deliver its full performance potential'. In practice, this means that it's normally rear-wheel drive, but when the rears lose traction power is fed to the fronts.

In addition to this, there's Super HICAS. In this system, sensors control the steering angle of the rear wheels by detecting yaw rate and monitoring both steering and accelerator inputs. It then decides on the correct rear-wheel steering input for best stability.

For the most skilful of professional racing drivers, this could all be considered a mollycoddling, fun-absorbing handicap, but the reality for the rest of us is a supremely controllable and well-balanced car.

When the tyres lose grip, you can feel it happen. Keep the power on and sure, you can feel the computers doing their stuff, correcting and adjusting just a little here and there, but ultimately the driver has control – certainly enough control (or lack of it) to go spinning off in a blur. Basically, the Skyline's electronics are certainly very clever but they still allowed us some very entertaining and accessible 'tarmacrobatics'.

Then, as the sun set behind a haze of near-Los Angelesian density and hungry midges came out in their trillions, we set off back to England. We filled up with petrol one last time (advantage Lotus) and droned back along the M4.

And droning is what this Esprit does, because despite there being a powerful, high-revving, multi-valve V8 just behind you, the noise it makes could never in a million years be mistaken for a Ferrari F355. A V6 Vectra sounds better, in fact even a Ford Puma makes a better racket. We'd be inclined to blame this on the sound-absorbing properties of the twin turbos, yet the Skyline, also a twin-turbo remember, manages to sound good 'n' grunty.

So, after two days of lashing and thrashing, what is the better high-performance answer? The Nissan gets the nod for reasons of practicality and finish. It has all the mod cons, too: four seats, good visibility and decent comfort. And, most important, it's still great fun to drive and bloody fast. And remember, with a bit of deft chippery and without excessive expense it can quite easily be made faster still.

But if we're talking pure, hedonistic sports use, the Esprit V8 GT is hard to beat. Yes, it's a pig to drive in traffic, and no, it doesn't have the practicality of the Nissan, but find a track and it is pretty well unbeatable. If we'd had this car at the Nürburgring last summer (issue 49) we're pretty confident it would have comfortably beaten the 911, the Corvette, the NSX, the M3, the Skyline, and maybe even the test-winning F355. High praise indeed □

BRAWN VERSUS BRAIN		
	Lotus Esprit V8 GT	Nissan Skyline GTR
Performance		
0-30mph (secs)	1.8	1.9
0-40mph (secs)	2.7	2.8
0-50mph (secs)	3.6	4.1
0-60mph (secs)	4.5	5.4
0-100kph (62mph)	n/a	5.7
0-70mph (secs)	6.0	6.9
0-80mph (secs)	7.4	9.2
0-90mph (secs)	8.8	11.3
0-100mph (secs)	10.8	13.7
0-110mph (secs)	12.8	17.1
0-120mph (secs)	14.9	20.8
0-130mph (secs)	18.7	25.4
Max speed (mph)	170 (limited)	155 (limited)
Standing 1/4 mile (secs)	12.7	14.0
Terminal speed (mph)	110.6	101.3
30-50mph in 3rd	2.8	4.5
30-50mph in 4th	4.6	7.0
50-70mph in 5th	6.2	10.2
30-70mph thru' gears	4.2	5.0
Braking, 70-0mph (metres/ft)	49.2/161.4	47.7/156.6
Costs		
On the road price	£49,950	£50,000
Test/combined mpg	20.1/21.2	18.4/n/a
Insurance group	20	20
Major service interval (miles)	6,000	18,000
Warranty (yrs/miles)	1/unltd	3/60,000
Equipment		
Airbag driver/passenger	£1,460/no	yes/yes
Alarm/immobiliser	£210/yes	yes/yes
ABS/Power steering	yes/yes	yes/yes
Air conditioning/Sunroof	£1,185/yes (removable)	yes/no
Elec windows/remote cent locking	yes/yes	yes/yes
Radio cassette/CD stacker	£445/£820	yes/yes
Technical		
Engine	V8cyl, 32v, dohc	in-line 6cyl, 24v dohc
	twin turbo	twin turbo
Capacity (cc)	3,508	2,568
Max power (bhp @ rpm)	349/6,500	276/6,800
Max torque (lb/ft @ rpm)	295/4,250	271/4,400
Transmission	5sp manual, rwd	5sp man, active
		4WD & 4WS
Brakes (f&r)	vented discs, ABS	vented discs, ABS
Suspension (f&r)	dble wishbones/multilink	multilink/multilink
Wheels	8.5Jx17 (f), 10Jx18 (r)	9Jx17
Tyres	235/40 ZR17 (f),	245/45 R17
	285/35 ZR18 (r) Michelin	Bridgestone
Kerb weight (kg)	1,340	1,540
Dimensions L/W (mm)	4,369/1,883	4,675/1,780

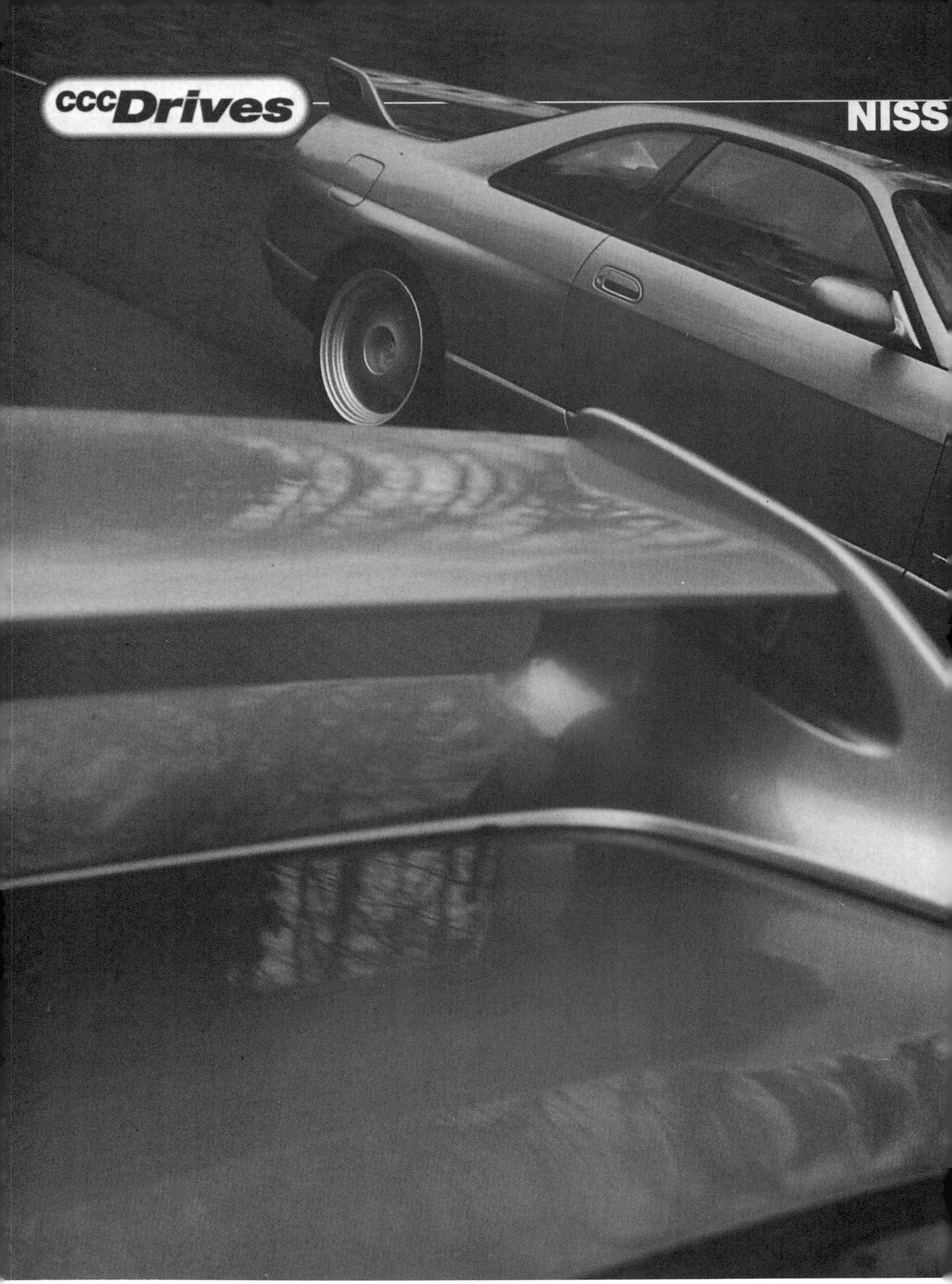

Big Boy's Toys

Big, brutal and twin turbocharged, the Skyline GTR is Japan's original supercar. But, as Steve Bennett discovers, just don't expect everyone to be impressed

Now I've driven all sorts of flash motors, but this has definitely never happened to me before. Picking my way through the chaos of Croydon's Tramlink dug-up one-way system, acclimatising myself to the sheer size of Nissan's Godzilla-like Skyline, the car behind beeps and flashes. Strange, I think, all the lights are functioning and I can only go as fast as what's in front of me - which isn't very.

Still maybe this person's in a hurry, so I move over. The Pug 306 pulls along side and the not unattractive young lady driver looks over, grins, and makes a sort of waggling gesture with her little finger before zipping off. It took a couple of moments to sink in but I believe such a gesture is designed to suggest that I am perhaps lacking somewhat in the trouser department!

Now I have to admit that it took a little while to see the humourous side but in retrospect I had to admit that it was quite funny (stop sniggering at the back), astute even. I'm treading on dangerous ground here, but take all that willy substitute

It takes a lot of provocation to get the Skyline to do this. Oh, and a snapper demanding a bit of drama

The beefy steering tells you just how much grip is available, while all that active differy is hard at work distributing the power perfectly

business that people like to apply to big fast cars, and the Nissan Skyline is it. It is motorised testosterone, all bulging with bumps and scoops and wings and stuff that make men go all sort of macho and women just laugh at. So there you go. Barely a quarter of a mile into my week-long Skyline experience and I had already been well and truly humiliated. Well, either that or she happened to know me!

Brushing aside the Freud stuff (quickly I think), the Skyline GTR is a car that we've kind of been waiting to get our mitts on. I say 'kind of' because there has been a Jap Supercar overload going on in the motoring press of late. But that's hardly surprising, since so much good stuff is coming out of Japan for us hard-driving chaps. The Skyline, though, is the daddy of them all. It actually has a fair bit of heritage, certainly more than those johnny-come-lately Subarus and Mitsubishi Evos.

The first Skyline GTR was conceived way back in 1969 for domestic motorsport use, where it was a big hit. Unfortunately it went a bit wrong in the '70s, when Nissan (or Datsun as they were then called) applied the name to all sorts of lacklustre saloons. In the '80s however, the Skyline was a force to reckoned with in Group A saloons. It was particularly strong in Japan and Australia, where it came close to winning at Bathurst.

Then Nissan launched the R32 Skyline and the legend really started to get moving. The R32 looks much like the current model and pioneered the intelligent four-wheel drive system and twin turbo straight-six for which the Skyline is now famous. The R32 is the car which became famous for breaking the production car lap record at the Nürburgring (although Caterham reckon they'll hold it now with a Superlight R).

It was a feat that was covered by most of the mainstream motoring mags of the day, fuelling the cult following and starting a steady stream of personal imports. The Skyline is no longer a racer, as there isn't much for it to race in since the known universe went 2.0-litre touring. It now just sort of exists. Not that it stops Nissan from launching new, even better models every year. And jolly good for them, we say!

Spot the difference? On the right is the boring standard engine. On the left we have the rooting, tooting 580bhp version with some serious mods

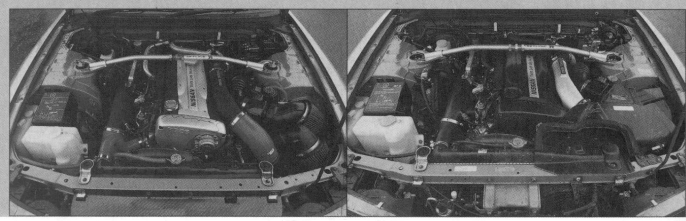

"It took a couple of moments to sink in, but I believe such a gesture is designed to suggest that I am, perhaps, lacking somewhat in the trouser department"

Above: an imposing sight. Right: Skyline was a formidable machine in National Saloons, with late Kieth Odor

And the current model, the car that my admirer was so impressed with, is the GTR V-spec. You can even buy it officially in this country now, although you'll have to quick since the UK's ration is rather meagre. And while the ration may be meagre, the price is a Skyline, sky high £50,000. But don't worry too much because second-hand import jobs cost less than half that and there's no shortage of specialists who will look after it for you. Having said that, they have a reputation for being totally bomb-proof, particularly in the standard 277bhp form.

But most owners consider 277bhp to be rather sluggish and Skyline tuning has become a big numbers game. It's hardly surprising really, when the standard car is effectively de-tuned and the only limit to horsepower seems to be what the bottom end will handle from the force-feeding twin turbos! The other GTR that we have on hand here is putting out a whopping 580bhp, but more on that after we've tamed the standard car!

Supplied courtesy of Nissan GB, this V-spec GTR feels good from the word go. The driving position is perfect, the steering wheel is just right, as are the pedals and gear lever position. All these things are important if you're going to feel relaxed and confident in what is a bit of a weapon. Once you're happy with all this, it's time to press the go button and again the Skyline doesn't disappoint – it sounds awesome! Move off and the GTR shows its intent immediately. Before I'd even made it out of the car park, the steering had wriggled and tram-lined and the suspension had started to gently massage my back. This was going to be fun!

A weapon is probably the best way to describe the Skyline. It does, after all, pack about as much

technology as some of those cruise missiles that have been buzzing Baghdad recently. In V-spec form it positively bristles with techy and strange abbreviations. For a start there's the ATTESA-ETS PRO four-wheel drive system. This uses a computer-controlled active rear diff (which features twin oil coolers, by the way) to switch from rear drive to 50/50 front and rear drive. In can do this in less than 1/100th of a second, getting you out of trouble as quickly as you get into it. The master brain can also transfer power to any individual wheel.

What else? Well, there's the SUPER HICAS III rear-wheel steering system which banishes understeer on turn-in and promotes oversteer on exit with the help of an active yaw control. The Mitsubishi Evo 5 comes with something similar. Now all this might sound as if you are just a passenger as the Skyline knuckles down and does it all for you. Fortunately, that is not the case. The Skyline is a great car to drive. Obviously, it handles. In fact, it handles like nothing else.

The beefy steering tells you just how much grip is available, while all that active differy is hard at work distributing the power perfectly – not just for power but for handling, too. And you can feel it all ►

Oh dear, more showing off from the Editor. Look it's not big and it's not clever

NISSAN SKYLINE GTR V-SPEC

SPECIFICATION

Engine:	2.6-litre, in-line six, twin turbo
Bore/stroke:	86mm x 73.7mm
Compression ratio:	10.4:1
Max power:	276bhp @ 6800rpm
Max torque:	271lb.ft @ 4400rpm
Transmission	Five-speed manual, intelligent 4wd
Front suspension:	Independent, multi-link, coil springs, anti-roll bar
Rear suspension:	Independent, multi-link, coil springs, anti-roll bar
Steering:	Super HICAS 4WS, pas
Brakes:	Brembo vented discs, 4-pot front, 2-pot rear
Wheels:	9Jx17in alloy
Tyres:	245/45 ZR17 Bridgestone
Power-to-weight:	166bhp per ton

PERFORMANCE

0-60mph:	5.38sec
Top speed:	150mph

happening, through your hands on the wheel, through the seat of your pants. But the beauty is that it's working for you and with you, not taking over.

What happens when you start to push the outer limits of the GTR's ability? Big, exploitable four-wheel drifts. Really dial the power in and you can slide around to your heart's content, although in the dry you'll be hard pushed to break any sort of traction. In the wet however, there's big fun to be had on roundabouts or even the handling circle at the Chobham test track. For maximum effect, hook second and apply a whole dollop of twin turbo boost at 4000rpm and then watch the tyres light up! Big fun!

Strangely, the Skyline doesn't actually feel that quick. It doesn't have that ballistic slug of mid-range that smaller turbo motors deliver. Instead, it just seems to build momentum in keeping with its size. The engine redlines at 8000rpm but you don't really need to go that far, as maximum power arrives at 6800rpm.

Instead, for seriously rapid but relaxed progress, change at about 5500rpm where the boost is really starting to swell up. The torque figures confirm the feeling, delivering a peak of 271lb.ft at 4400rpm. But we do, of course, have something up our sleeves in the power department. Enter Nick Paddy and his rocket ship of a Skyline!

Big, big power

Whatever way you look at it, 580bhp is a very big number indeed. But like we said, Skyline tuning knows few boundaries except fiscal ones. Nick runs a business called GTR Performance that specialises in some major Skyline tuning parts. Naturally, his two-year old pre-V-spec GTR reflects this, being fully loaded and painstakingly developed. We had to try it.

This sort of power comes from some very heavy breathing mods. Bigger HKS roller bearing turbos with large bore down pipes are used. The inlet and exhaust manifolds are extensively polished and ported, along with the cylinder head which features Mines fast road cams with adjustable vernier pulleys. A bigger Mines airflow meter plus 600cc injectors and a HKS high-flow fuel pump makes sure that enough of the combustion mixture makes it to the chambers. You can expect 8mpg and a fuel gauge that you can actually see going down when the boost is up.

A huge alloy intercooler and air induction kit further aid the process and, naturally, a rather different ECU is employed. Amazingly, the bottom end is standard. All the engine work was carried out round the corner from the **CCC** offices, at Croydon's Abbey Motorsport.

Six-pot AP callipers for serious track day work

Gearbox is actually standard although Nick has reservations about its ability to handle such power and changes at 6000rpm. The clutch is a twin-plate job but with a modified clutch arm to give it a similar feel to standard. AP six-pot callipers replace the standard four-pot Brembos at the front which Nick reckons can't handle track day abuse.

Boost is controlled via a Trust digital boost controller hidden in the ashtray, while an exhaust temperature gauge likes in the glove compartment. The full 580bhp arrives with 1.4bar dialled in, although only for 15 seconds – Nick describes it as his overtaking button! A more sedate 480bhp is maintained at 1.2bar and 0.9bar is selected when Nick's girlfriend gets behind the wheel (so he says).

So how quick is quick? Given that it was wet, we didn't go too mad, but I did experience boost at all three settings and, quite honestly, each was bloody fast. Interestingly, more boost didn't seem to mean more lag and the difference between 0.9 and 1.4bar is a different degree of blur as the scenery starts to go backwards. Seriously, it is devastatingly fast and flexible, with the power really coming on from 3000rpm. And so smooth. No Cosworth-style banging and popping, just a huge gob of power.

Nick reckons that even on 1.4bar it is serious overkill on the road. Things just start to happen too quickly and there isn't enough time to react. He uses it mainly as a track day machine and sticks slicks on it. The Nürburgring and Spa are on the calendar for this year.

Impressive indeed, but equally impressive was the suspension package. The standard car is too hard for our pot-holed roads and boy, does it tramline. Nicks car uses an off the shelf, fully adjustable Quantum set-up (Quantum supply many of the BTCC teams) and it really does transform the ride and handling. Unfortunately, it's also fearsomely expensive, although Nick has commissioned Leda to come up with a suspension package for the British market.

Aftermath

So where does the Skyline fit in with the current generation of rally-derived supercars? Truth be told, it is rather as it looks: a bit of a dinosaur, albeit of the Godzilla fantasy variety. Cars like the Impreza and the Mitsubishi Evo are more nimble, probably more usable and certainly less intimidating – plus they have rally heritage. The GTR is more a Mad Max road racer, the car they would cast for the re-make. Personally I loved it, but I'm not sure that I liked what other people thought. But you know what they say, size isn't everything. □

Japan's fastest coupe, perhaps the world's fastest coupe, has just got faster. As reported last month, the amazing computer-controlled, four-wheel-driven and four-wheel-steered Nissan Skyline GT-R has had a serious all-over revamp.

Aside from the obvious revised styling, its length and wheelbase have been trimmed and its width marginally increased, while its height has been left untouched. Whichever way you twist it the new R34's chassis is at least 50 per cent stiffer and the new body and underside have revised aerodynamics.

Under the bonnet there's the familiar in-line six-cylinder 2.6-litre twin turbo from the previous R33 model. But although there's no extra horsepower in standard trim, due to Japan's domestic powercapping – it remains the same at 276bhp – an all-new Garret turbocharger and an increased compression ratio have increased peak torque from 271 to 289lb ft.

In addition a new gearbox, (co-developed with Getrag), now has a sixth ratio and various major suspension components have been lightened through use of aluminium, stiffened and/or wholly redesigned. The wheels, for example, are each a kilo lighter and up from 17 to 18 inches in diameter with lower profile 245/40 tyres.

Once behind the wheel I first noticed that the front bucket seats offer more lateral support and they're more comfortable too. The first improvement to come to light while on the move is that the new turbo provides better throttle response at low to medium speeds, with enough acceleration to give you a thump in the back at almost any engine speed. The motor spins more freely right up to its 8,000rpm rev limit and there's no drop-off in torque even at those high revs.

The new gearbox changes more smoothly than the old and, with the improved torque and better-placed ratios, 0-62mph acceleration has improved from the R33's 5.4secs to 4.9secs, which in turn is just a whisker

NISSAN SKYLINE GT-R R34
Sky's the limit

off the old GT-R's time of 4.7secs when 'chipped' up to 350bhp.

Although there's still a degree of tramlining on poor surfaces, the R34 gives even less feeling of speed than the previous model. This can be explained by new front and rear air-diffusers, coupled with the top V-spec model's new two-tier rear wing, which at around 110mph bestow the R34 with healthy downforce. But even at 60mph the car's aerodynamics give it road-holding on a par with a magnetised slot car and in a corner it is the most stable car I have ever driven.

Another welcome improvement is the R34's reduced understeer. Providing you're smooth with the steering the new car turns in without the tyres scrubbing and its nose running wide. The brakes have been uprated too, with more power and feel coupled with reduced fade under hard use.

Nissan has confirmed that during recent tests at the 12.9-mile Nürburgring circuit, the R34 has lapped quicker than the previous production car record set by the old Skyline GT-R, but because they weren't going for a record, an official time has yet to be released. Rumour has it that the new car may already be up to 10secs a lap faster...

A decision has yet to be made as to whether the R34 will be officially imported into the UK, but if it is it'll cost at least £50,000 (around £30,000 in Japan). So if you have that amount to spare, would 11mpg (which I managed on this test) bother you too much? I wouldn't complain □

Story Yasushi Ishiwatari
Photography Takahito Naitoh

FACT FILE	
Model	two-door coupe
Engine	2.6-litre, 6-cyl twin turbo, 276bhp
Performance	0-62 in 4.9secs, 155mph
Price	approx £27,990 in Japan
On sale in the UK	to be or not to be?
Rivals	Subaru Impreza 22B,
	Mitsubishi Evo 6
Likes	everything except
Dislikes	fuel consumption

V-SPECIAL

DRIVE NISSAN SKYLINE GTR The pared-down, pumped-up R34 version of the Skyline hits British roads for the first time. And it's more thrilling than ever. By Stephen Sutcliffe

t's wise to take a minute – maybe even five – before you attempt to unravel the new Skyline GTR. Approach it as you would a normal car and you'll almost certainly miss the point. What you'll see is a car that very obviously comes from the East, wears a ridiculously over-the-top set of skirts and spoilers and sports a pair of blistered rear wheel arches that, despite their girth, only just manage to contain the enormous wheels and tyres that lurk within. What you'll see is a hot rod, pure and simple.

But, of course, you know that the new R34 Nissan Skyline GTR V-Spec is no hot rod. You know it's a car that fizzes with technology, even though you've not yet driven it. It's a bit like the assumption you make about what goes on behind closed doors at NASA; you've never actually been inside, but you don't imagine there are too many people stoking coal fires and discussing their preferred brand of pork pie in there.

What you're unlikely to grasp without actually driving this car is how subtly the technology is applied, and how sweetly it comes at you through the steering, seats and chassis. But the fact that the R34 is based on the wonderful and astonishingly capable R33 GTR – and follows very closely in its footsteps – should make you suspect as much.

Most of the latest Skyline's technical make-up is, in fact, not new but redesigned. The straight-six twin-turbo engine is a development of the old 2.6-litre unit, for example, and shares the same capacity and official power output of 277bhp at 6800rpm – though unofficially this figure is said to be nearer 320bhp.

The chassis, too, though a little lighter and leaner than before, still serves up the same irresistible recipe: multi-link suspension fore and aft, aided in no small measure by Nissan's HICAS four-wheel steering and a computer-controlled four-wheel-drive system which takes into account steering angle, yaw rate, throttle opening and probably the temperature inside your underwear in order to direct just the right amount of torque to whichever axle needs it.

The big difference this time around is that the software for the four-wheel-drive system is

Still the sliding supremo; few four-wheel-drive cars are this adjustable

Gearbox now has six gears; seven separate LCD graphs on console screen

about twice as clever as before. There's also a much improved set of Brembo anchors (bigger discs and beefier calipers) plus an extra cog in the new Getrag-designed six-speed gearbox.

If you clamber underneath the car you'll also spot two suspiciously space age-looking fillets of carbon fibre – one beneath the engine, the other under the rear axle line. Each is designed to ease airflow over the bits that would otherwise poke out beneath the car; the idea is to eliminate lift, though I'd hate to think how much they'd cost to replace after

you'd thumped the bottom of your brand new GTR into a sleeping policeman.

Climb inside the Skyline and twist the titanium key in the ignition. Listen to the straight six crank up, then settle into a familiar hum-rumble at its 1000rpm idle. And it's difficult not to smirk as the LCD display on the dash comes to life. To begin with it just reads "Skyline GTR", but after a couple of seconds this fades to reveal seven separate bar graphs that deliver real-time information on boost pressure, throttle opening, injector pressure, and temperatures ◗

Outrageous spoilers and skirts contribute to hot rod look; huge wheel arches barely contain new 18-inch alloys

◆ for oil, water, exhaust and cabin. Blip the throttle and the graphs do a little dance to the rhythm of your right foot. You can even dial up a digital turbo boost gauge that provides a constant 30sec telemetry read-out, just so you can be sure the blowers aren't letting the side down.

Of arguably greater significance are the new seats, which hold you in an even more vice-like grip than before, and which feature two holes in the backrest to allow you to fit a full racing harness.

The steering wheel is chunkier and better to hold than you remember, while the pedals are absolutely where you want them. So while Nissan's interior designers may well have been allowed to consume just a little too much sake at work – hence the polka dot seat cover design and the strips of fake titanium around the gear lever and heater controls – it hasn't affected the superb ergonomics. Getting into a Skyline still feels like you've climbed aboard a racing car in which the focus is all on how comfortable you, the driver, can get behind the wheel.

It's raining when we finally rumble off down the road, waving goodbye to the car's owner, in search of somewhere to drive and photograph his precious new £50,000 toy. Perfect Skyline weather.

The first thing that strikes me is the ride; it's noticeably calmer and quieter than the old car's.

Ruts and ripples that sent great crashes and bangs through the R33 GTR I'd arrived in an hour ago are dealt with much more effectively. And although there's still a discernible whine from the big 245/40 18-inch Bridgestone RE040 tyres as they rumble across the same wet tarmac, it's nothing like as pronounced as it was on the way here.

One of the old GTR's biggest weaknesses was its almost laughable turbo lag. Open the throttle wide at any crank speed below 4000rpm and you could just about sing the national anthem before anything meaningful happened at the wheels. In this car, despite the fact that Nissan has been open enough to put smaller markings on the revcounter up to 3000rpm, with wider-spaced calibrations appearing between there and the 8000rpm red line, it is immediately apparent that there is less lag. A lot less.

Following our camera car out of the city centre I wind the accelerator right open in a high gear just to see when the action starts, and even by 2500rpm the familiar whooshes of two turbos about to deliver their haymakers can be heard.

By 2800rpm the rapidly swelling numbers on the bar

Feels breathtakingly fast despite turbo lag; red line is heady 8000rpm

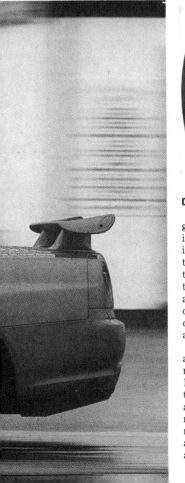

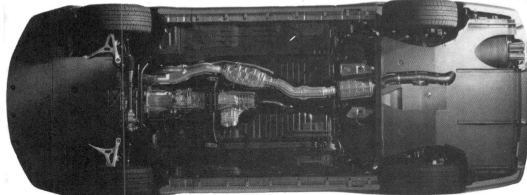

Carbon fibre panels underneath engine and rear axle reduce high-speed lift; multi-link suspension front and rear

graph confirm the subjective impression that hyperspace is imminent. So I back off and there's a distant chatter from the wastegates as they dump the boost pressure that was about to spear us into the back of the car ahead. God it feels quick – and I haven't even gone above 40mph yet.

Skylines have always felt amazingly tough from a mechanical point of view, and I'm glad to report that not a thing has changed. Skimming across these streaming wet roads there's something very reassuring about the meatiness and accuracy from the steering and brakes, and about the way ▶

Twin-turbo 2.6 officially rated at 277bhp; real output probably over 300bhp

◆ the car just feels so planted, even at modest speeds. It makes you feel terribly secure about driving a Skyline. It just feels very, very strong. Even the gearchange has an unburstable feel, despite the shift being shorter, crisper and more precise than before.

A short section of dual carriageway and the bloke in the Calibra can't quite believe what he's seeing: a brand new Skyline GTR doing no more than 30mph, and some lunatic leaning out of the car in front pointing a camera at it. Why doesn't he put his foot down, I can see our friend in the Calibra thinking. So I do. And as the revs rise past 3000rpm the Skyline pulls itself together and delivers the most graphic example of the difference between fast cars and supercars that I have experienced in a long time.

For a second the Vauxhall draws alongside, but as soon as the Nissan's lungs are filled it doesn't just drive away, it disappears. Gone, leaving photographer Stan Papior almost as confused as our friend in the Calibra. Sorry Stan, but I couldn't resist.

Yes, it's quick, this new Skyline. Notably quicker than the old car, which we timed at 5.0sec to 60mph, 13.0sec to 100mph and 156mph flat out. The top speed won't have changed because it's still limited, but I'd make an educated guess of 60mph in 4.5sec and 100mph in 11.0sec. To match it you would need a BMW M5, which requires a piggy bank able to provide an extra £10,000.

But as you may already know, straight-line speed has never been the Skyline's key virtue. That was always its handling and grip – and its consequent ability to get from A to B faster than any other car in the universe, save the mighty Mitsubishi Evo VI.

Nissan claims that a number of factors make the new GTR considerably quicker across country than its predecessor. There's talk of an official

Exterior styling all new, but details like huge circular tail lights mean it is clearly part of GTR bloodline; calibrations on revcounter wider past 3000rpm

New car should demolish 0-60mph sprint in less than 5.0sec; maximum speed is still limited to 112mph

ide much better resolved; big mid-corner bumps no longer threaten GTR

ub-7min 55sec lap around the Nürburgring, which would make about 30sec faster by our eckoning. The main reason, part from the sophistication of s four-wheel-drive system, is he reduction in weight and ulk. The new car is about 60kg ghter and a little smaller in all irections, which should make it ven more agile on the road.

But not, perhaps, by as much as you'd think. On public roads differences in agility between old and new exist, yes, but they're pretty subtle. The new GTR still feels like a big barge to drive quickly on non-dual carriageway UK roads, even though its body control and general agility are better than before.

What does make a difference is the extra feel through the

steering and brakes, and the fact that the damping is better able to deal with the sort of mid-corner ruts that would occasionally bounce the R33 off line.

I was also a bit worried that Nissan might have removed from the programme the old car's ability to deliver delicious wet-weather power slides – the sort that no Audi quattro driver could ever contemplate. That was one of the things that made the R33 unique among four-wheel-drive cars.

But I needn't have fretted. You can be even more spectacular in the new car, despite its deeper reserves of power, torque, stability, control and cross-country speed.

Some things never change, it seems. And in the case of the new Skyline, that's just how it should be. More of the same, only better. ⊙

FACTFILE

NISSAN SKYLINE GTR

HOW MUCH?	
Price	£50,000 (est)
On sale	Not in UK

HOW FAST?	
0-62mph	4.5sec (est)
Top speed	112mph (limited)

HOW THIRSTY?	
Japanese standard	22.8mpg

HOW BIG?	
Length	4600mm
Width	1785mm
Height	1360mm
Wheelbase	2665mm
Weight	1560kg
Fuel tank	65 litres

ENGINE	
Layout	6 cyls in line, 2568cc
Max power	277bhp at 6800rpm
Max torque	293lb ft at 4400rpm
Specific output	108bhp per litre
Power to weight	177bhp per tonne
Installation	Longitudinal, front, four-wheel drive
Made of	Alloy head, iron block
Bore/stroke	86.0/73.7mm
Compression ratio	8.5:1
Valve gear	4 per cyl, dohc
Ignition and fuel	Sequential electronic fuel injection

GEARBOX	
Type	6-speed manual
Ratios/mph per 1000rpm	
1st 3.83/5.6	2nd 2.36/9.1
3rd 1.69/12.8	4th 1.31/16.4
5th 1.00/21.5	6th 0.79/27.3
Final drive 3.55	

SUSPENSION	
Front	Multi-link, coil springs and dampers, anti-roll bar
Rear	Multi-link, coil springs and dampers, anti-roll bar

STEERING	
Type	Rack and pinion, power assisted
Lock to lock 2.9	

BRAKES	
Front	Ventilated discs
Rear	Ventilated discs
Anti-lock	Standard

WHEELS AND TYRES	
Size	18in
Made of	Cast alloy
Tyres	245/40 ZR18

Figures are manufacturer's claims

VERDICT
Smaller, sportier Skyline GTR builds on strengths of previous model. Electrifying performance with involving handling.

Skyline's

Japan's famous hi-tech terror creature is re-born, stronger

new limit

...en more capable. *PETER NUNN hung on for the ride of his life*

With stronger torque,

a new six-speed box plus the usual GT-R attributes of **phenomenal 4WD traction** and stopping power, the GT-R again qualifies as a simply **fantastic** driver's car

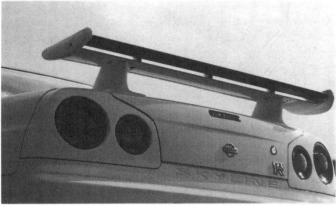

Forget WRXs and Lancer Evos.

Honda's S2000 isn't in it, either. The true heavy hitter in Japan right now, the car everyone is talking about, is the new R34 Nissan Skyline GT-R. Real-world *Gran Turismo*. A car with shattering speed that feels hewn from solid metal. Ten years on from the R32 that re-invented the Skyline GT-R myth in Japan, Godzilla is again upsetting applecarts.

Okay, so this R34 might not go down in history as the best-looking of the modern GT-R breed, but it is unquestionably the best sorted. As it should be, seeing as it's '99 state-of-the-art and has been lovingly bolted together by squads of die-hard Nissan engineers.

They spent long hours camped out at the Nurburgring in Germany working on the new 2.6 litre twin turbo/4WD Godzilla, perfecting its many dynamic functions to the point where they found it could lap the legendary 20.832km circuit faster than any Japanese production car before it. So what, you might ask. Its predecessor, the R33 GT-R (born in 1995), was hailed as the first production car to break the 8min barrier around the Ring. The fact Nissan says the R34 can now lap the Teutonic track 30sec quicker points to all kinds of advances in engine, braking,

handling and roadholding.

In a straight line, the new Godzilla is not really so much faster than the old (Nissan claims 13.8sec for 0-400m, compared with 14.1sec for the R33, but we'll come back to that later). The point is, the new R34 communicates better at the helm. It's easier to place and, with tighter body and suspension control, Godzilla understeers less through the fast curvy bits. With stronger torque, new six-speed box plus the usual GT-R attributes of phenomenal 4WD traction and stopping power, the GT-R again qualifies as a simply fantastic driver's car.

Such is life, the Nurburgring wasn't on the menu this time. No worries. As well as day-to-day roads, we got to hammer the new GT-R around the 280km/h bowl at Japan's JARI research institute as well as up through the hills above Tsukuba, to the northwest of Tokyo, where it stormed the straights and turned in with a speed and balance that was astounding for a car of its size and bulk.

Previous GT-Rs were brilliant in fast sweepers but demanded rather more of your attention in tight corners. The R34 feels immediately wieldy and playful, the steering low-geared (just 2.6 turns

between locks) but wholly precise and full of feel. Weighty too, but then that's another GT-R characteristic that's part of the package, right?

Those who know their GT-Rs will recognise stronger front-end bite this time, those massive 18in wheels simply turning left or right to steering commands. The secret is hugely improved body rigidity. GT-R chief engineer Kouzo Watanabe says bending stiffness this time improves 56 percent while torsional rigidity doubles.

In slow-to-medium bends, the GT-R is now marvellously quick and (almost) Lotus-agile. While the R32 GT-R (and to a certain extent, the R33, too) could bite back if you suddenly backed off on the loud pedal mid-corner, this '99 Godzilla stays resolutely planted. It's the most accessible GT-R yet.

This user-friendliness is not just down to the new body structure. The GT-R crew has rebushed Godzilla's acclaimed multilink suspension and the Super HICAS four-wheel-steering electronics that check vehicle speed and steering input have also been

reprogrammed. Nissan talks airily about the 4WD now incorporating model-following control procedures of jet fighters, whatever that means.

Nissan has also come up with some serious rubber – massive 245/40 ZR 18 Bridgestone Potenza RE 40s. Specially developed for the car, they adorn one-piece forged 18in alloys (which save 16kg over the R33's 17 x 9JJ rims).

Godzilla now stands smaller on the road although, from the outside, eyeing up its brazen, muscled-up sheetmetal, you'd hardly guess. To reduce mass, Watanabe and his team have shortened the GT-R by 75mm and brought the front overhang back 20mm, too. The two-door shell is based off the new, downsized Skyline platform that debuted in Japan in mid '98. This also saves 55mm.

Fine, but having digested those numbers, the surprise is to find the GT-R still weighs the same. If anything, it's actually put on 10-20kg,

adjustable 'attack angle.'

When approaching the Skyline from behind, the rear flanks create a distinctive profile. Good or bad? You decide. As Skyline tradition demands there are, of course, those four distinctively round tail-lights. Up front, you get a massive bonnet under which resides that rumbling RB 26 DETT straight-six: Another integral part of modern GT-R folklore. All told, this is a brutal-looking car, a cousin of sorts to the BMW M Coupe.

Its twin cam 24-valve 2568 cm³ engine must redefine the word strong. For '99, this fabled warrior gets worked over again, with new cams for improved valve timing and a pair of twin ball bearing ceramic turbos for sharper throttle response.

When it comes to power, Nissan has again bowed to an industry 'understanding' in Japan and printed 280PS in the catalogue so as not to get Transport Ministry bureaucrats (who don't like 300bhp and above) all excited. Catalogues,

depending on which version you order. The standard car tips the scales at 1540kg while the V-Spec tested here is 1560kg.

V-spec? This is Nissan code for the GT-R's smarter twin brother, the difference this time round starting with aerodynamics. The V-spec gets underbody diffusers (front and rear) for increased downforce which, in turn, helps handling, grip and straight-line stability above 80km/h.

Both GT-Rs wear that massive, two-pronged aluminium boot spoiler with

Why bother to stir the cogs when the GT-R is flexible enough to *pull smoothly away* from 1000rpm in fourth? Impressive, that

however, have been known to give a fairly liberal interpretation of the truth... So with power officially capped, the other way to increase GT-R speed is through torque. The cams and ECU changes see pulling power upped 6.5 percent to a formidable new 392Nm at 4400 rpm. Torque of that order might seem to make gearchanging superfluous and around town, in traffic, you'd be right. Why bother to stir the cogs when the GT-R is flexible enough to pull smoothly away from 1000rpm in fourth? Impressive, that.

What helps is that Nissan has also brought a new six-speed Getrag box to the party. The effect of this is to lower the gearing and bring ratios one to five closer together. Sixth is out on a limb as an overdrive. Like

the whole car, this gearbox has a solid, heavy, very deliberate feel about it. In fact, it feels great. Start testing Godzilla G-forces and its monoform bucket seat (with side airbags) will hold you resolutely in place. Better still, it's actually quite comfortable.

Nissan has kept the cabin simple and to the point. Sturdy three-spoke wheel, conventional instruments, logical minor controls. It's all new gear, though. But Nissan couldn't resist doing a zillion-function LCD display atop the centre console, telling you *everything* about the car's mechanical workings. Front/rear torque split, boost pressure and oil and water temperature for starters. There's heaps more, like injector pressure, throttle angle, intake air temperature as well as routine

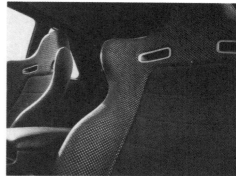

stuff like 3D real-time satellite-navigation.

The R34 comes with that familiar deep-seated growl that builds to a powerful, all-enveloping crescendo as the tacho needle starts to wind right. In the background, you hear a faint turbo whistle. Nissan has set the red line at 8000rpm again, but there is now a warning when you have 500 rpm to go. In truth, you really have to be pretty determined to seek out that final 1000rpm, because the engine is definitely happiest and does its best work between three and six grand. The turbo

boost is now strong and progressive; from 3000rpm up, the GT-R is really trucking on. While the R33 could feel laggy, the new Godzilla never does.

Authoritative test figures from Japan's *Car Graphic* magazine reveal the good-and-bad news. First, the bad news. Testing V-spec editions of R33 and R34, the old car proves quicker to 100 km/h (4.4sec vs 4.9sec) and for 0-400m, too (12.7sec vs 13.1sec). That wasn't in the script, surely, and certainly contradicts the Authorised Version from Nissan.

Where Godzilla, the new generation, scores is in third, fourth and fifth gear acceleration, especially at either ends of the scale like 20-40km/h and 140-160km/h. But figures show that, for flexibility, it's actually quicker right across the board. More likely, though, you'll be making full use of the box because it shifts so well (the gate is meaty yet precise) and the new close ratios let you keep Godzilla deliciously 'on the cams'.

The GT-R chassis is one of the most

sophisticated in the business and, on the GT-R V-spec seen here, the electronics not only vary the torque split, front-to-rear depending on how maniacally you drive it, but between right and left rear wheels, too. The whole system is then integrated with ABS.

For the most part, though, Godzilla acts like a good rear-driver. A tight corner, power on and it will let you kick the tail out. While the electronics are then scrambling to divert torque to the front axle, you wind off some lock to control the slide.

Not that Godzilla is perfect, mind. The suspension's pretty stiff and the ride is hard, becoming knobbly over patchy or broken surfaces. Ruts in the road can also cause the GT-R to tramline quite badly. Steering, for all its new accuracy, also brings a frustratingly wide turning circle. It's areas such as this where the mighty and magnificent GT-R still can't match the complete Carrera 4. But it remains the best *Gran Turismo* game you'll ever play.

Nissan Skyline GT-R V-spec	
Price	
Basic	$75,500 (app.)
Engine	
Layout	longitudinal inline 6, dohc, 24v
Induction	multi-point fuel injection, twin turbo charged
Capacity(litres)	2.568
Bore/stroke	86.0/ 763.7mm
Compression ratio	8.5:1
Maximum power	206kW@6800rpm
Maximum torque	392Nm@4400rpm
Redline/cut-out	8000rpm
Transmission	
Ratios	6-speed manual
First	3.827
Second	2.360
Third	1.685
Fourth	1.312
Fifth	1.000
Sixth	0.793
Differential ratio	3.266
Suspension	
Front	multilink, upper A-arms, lower links, coil springs, anti-roll bar
Rear	multilink, upper links, lower A-arms, coil springs, anti-roll bar
4WS	Super-HICAS with yaw rate feedback control
Tyres	245/40ZR18 Bridgestone Potenza RE 40
Brakes	
Front	vented discs, ABS
Rear	vented discs
Steering	
Steering type	power-assisted, rack and pinion
Turning circle (m)	10.2
Turns lock to lock	2.6
Vital Statistics	
Wheelbase	2665mm
Front track	1480mm
Rear track	1490mm
Length	4600mm
Width	1785mm
Height	1360mm
Weight	1540kg
Fuel tank	65 litres
Performance	
0-400m	13.8 sec (manufacturer's claim)
Top speed	180km/h (limited)

YUM AND YU

Few cars are as entertaining or as awesome point to point as Mitsubishi's Evo V

MMER

Except the latest Nissan Skyline GTR

MITSUBISHI EVO VI
PRICE £30,995 **TOP SPEED** 150mph **0-60MPH** 4.4sec
30-70MPH 4.1sec **60-0MPH** 2.5sec **MPG** 21.2

NISSAN SKYLINE GTR
PRICE £54,000 **TOP SPEED** 156mph **0-60MPH** 4.6sec
30-70MPH 3.9sec **60-0MPH** 2.5sec **MPG** 18.9

In March this year we published a road test of the mighty Mitsubishi Evo VI, and at the end of the test we awarded it a rare five-star rating, closing with the words: "This car is entirely beyond compare in our experience."

We weren't joking, either. Due to its mind-bending combination of rocket-sled performance, track car handling, rugged good looks and untouchable value for money, the £31,000, 150mph Evo VI completely rewrote the rule book on fast cars.

Now, however, the time has come for the Evo VI to really show us its mettle. Because here, for the first time ever, the Mitsubishi meets the awesome new Nissan Skyline R34 GTR back to back on UK roads.

The Nissan is hugely more expensive at £54,000 and isn't available officially in the UK until next year. But in reality you just know that these two were made to go head to head. We just had to know which is best.

STAN PAPIOR AND TIM WREN

DESIGN & ENGINEERING

It is hard to think of two other cars that contain more technology than this pair. Yet despite their perceived similarities, there are a number of technical differences that separate them.

For starters, the Evo VI was essentially conceived to win rallies, and as a result it owes almost every trick it possesses to motorsport. The Skyline, on the other hand, has never been anything other than a pure road car, a philosophy to which the new R34 remains faithful. But the fact that many owners have subsequently taken to the track in their Skylines is testament to the versatility of the design.

They are also very different in terms of size and weight. The Nissan is 5-series big, the Evo slightly smaller than a 3-series. On the road, this disparity is bound to affect their relative performance, especially since officially they produce near identical amounts of power: Nissan 277bhp at 6800rpm, Mitsubishi 276bhp at 6500rpm. Unofficially, however, the Nissan has nearer 320bhp, which puts it right up beside the Evo on power to weight.

Although the new Skyline may look leaner and lighter than its predecessor, technically it is little more than an evolution of the now legendary R33 GTR. So while it has shrunk by 75mm in length and has a 55mm shorter wheelbase, its powertrain is a development of the R33's.

The straight-six engine is virtually unchanged apart from the fitment of two new ceramic Garrett turbochargers and an uprated intercooler. A new exhaust system and lightweight sodium-filled exhaust valves have improved torque and throttle response slightly. There is now 289lb ft at 4400rpm compared with 271lb ft at 4400rpm for the R33. But otherwise the 2.6-litre block is unaltered from the one that first appeared 10 years ago.

What is new is the six-speed gearbox, a joint development between Nissan and Getrag. With closer ratios, it promises to plug the hole in the five-speed car's laggy off-boost response.

As before, the R34 features an electronic four-wheel-drive system, complete with active limited-slip differential. In normal circumstances this allows 100 per cent of the torque to go through the rear wheels, but as much as 50 per cent of this can be transferred

MITSUBISHI EVO VI 1 Momo wheel looks and feels low-rent beside Skyline item 2 Speedometer converted to miles per hour, now reads to 180mph 3 Adjustable under-thigh support for terrific bucket seats 4 Evo has only five forward cogs, but quick-shift change is a delight 5 Red line set at 7000rpm but engine will go to 7800rpm before limiter intrudes 6 Air conditioning standard, but stereo is a dealer option

Evo's 2.0-litre four-cylinder engine is laggier than the Skyline's six but is an even bigger mid-range haymaker

Extreme provocation and plenty of room required to get Evo to do this. On the road, it either grips or understeers

NISSAN SKYLINE GTR 1 New Getrag/Nissan-developed six-speed gearbox has plugged the hole in old car's off-boost mid-range lethargy. Change action is meaty, precise **2** Leather wheel feels as good as it looks **3** Seats covered in Connolly leather on all 100 GTRs to be sold through Nissan GB **4** Computer atop dash is great gimmick to begin with **5** Titanium-look plastic on console is of high quality **6** CD changer is standard

GTR's 2.6-litre twin-turbo engine is a development of old car's: official power is 277bhp, unofficially it's 320bhp

Skyline's chassis is much more adjustable than Mitsubishi's on the limit. Steering feel and grip are better, too

to the front if the sensors on the steering, brakes, throttle and wheels detect slip. The latest Skyline also features an uprated four-wheel steering system and has bigger brake calipers than before.

In contrast to the Skyline, the Evo has a marginally less potent single-turbo 2.0-litre four-cylinder engine that drives through a five-speed gearbox. It is also permanent four-wheel drive rather than part-time, with the natural torque split set at 50/50.

The one trick the Evo has up its sleeve is its active yaw system, which operates via the front and rear diffs to effectively eliminate under and oversteer. Like the GTR, it has all-round disc brakes that are fitted with anti-lock.

Evo is lighter, but GTR is more high-tech	
MITSUBISHI	★★★★★
NISSAN	★★★★★

PERFORMANCE, BRAKES

All out against the stopwatch, there is never more than a tenth or two in it on acceleration. The shorter geared and lighter Evo VI initially feels more explosive, hence its marginal superiority up to about 80mph. But beyond this it's the torquier Skyline that starts to edge away, eventually pipping the Evo to 100mph with a devastating time of 10.8sec (Evo 11.2sec). And it is the Skyline that is quicker from 30-70mph, thanks mainly to the fact that it will do 70mph in second whereas the Evo needs an extra gearchange just to make 60mph. The Skyline also has the greater top speed: 156mph against 150mph.

What is most fascinating is the different approaches they employ in order to obtain almost identical results. The Evo is noisier and more frenetic, and suffers from more turbo lag than the Skyline. But when it goes, it goes even harder than the Nissan. Its mid-range pick-up is eye-watering once the turbo is at full pressure beyond 2700rpm. And although the Skyline feels ludicrously rapid by ordinary standards, beside the Evo its acceleration never feels quite as dramatic.

Part of this is down to the fact that the Evo has nothing like as much sound deadening as the Skyline, which heightens the impression of speed and drama compared with the quieter, calmer, more mature ◗

MITSUBISHI EVO VI

ENGINE
Layout 4 cyls in line, 1997cc
Max power 276bhp at 6500rpm
Max torque 274lb ft at 3000rpm
Specific output 138bhp per litre
Power to weight 202bhp per tonne
Torque to weight 201lb ft per tonne
Installation Front, transverse, four-wheel drive
Construction Aluminium head and block
Bore/stroke 85.0/88.0mm
Valve gear 4 valves per cyl, dohc
Compression ratio 8.8:1
Ignition and fuel Mitsubishi ECi ignition, sequential injection, Mitsubishi turbocharger with water-cooled intercooler

GEARBOX
Type 5-speed manual by Mitsubishi
Ratios/mph per 1000rpm
1st 2.78/5.9 **2nd** 1.95/8.4
3rd 1.41/11.6 **4th** 1.03/15.9
5th 0.76/21.6
Final drive ratio 4.53

SUSPENSION
Front MacPherson struts, lower wishbones, coil springs, anti-roll bar, active yaw
Rear Multi-link, coil springs, anti-roll bar, active yaw

STEERING
Type Rack and pinion, power assisted
Turns lock to lock 2.6

BRAKES
Front 332mm ventilated discs
Rear 306mm ventilated discs
Anti-lock Standard

WHEELS AND TYRES
Wheel size 7.5Jx17in
Made of Cast alloy
Tyres 225/45 ZR17 Bridgestone S-01
Spare Space saver

MITSUBISHI EVO VI

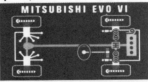

VITAL STATISTICS
Body 4dr saloon **Cd** 0.36 **Front/rear tracks** 1510/1505mm **Turning circle** 11.0m **Min/max front leg room** 850/1070mm **Max front head room** 1010mm **Min/max rear leg room** 580/810mm **Max rear head room** 910mm **Interior width front/rear** 1420/1410mm **VDA boot volume** 420 litres **Kerb weight** 1365kg **Weight f/r** 58/42 per cent **Width (inc mirrors)** 1875mm

FUEL CONSUMPTION

TEST RESULTS — Mitsubishi Evo VI / Nissan Skyline GTR

GOVERNMENT CLAIMS
Mitsubishi Evo VI — Tank: 60 litres (13.2 galls) Range: 390 miles
Nissan Skyline GTR — Tank: 65 litres (14.3 galls) Range: 350 miles

---

NISSAN SKYLINE GTR

ENGINE
Layout 6 cyls in line, 2568cc
Max power 277bhp at 6800rpm
Max torque 293lb ft at 4400rpm
Specific output 108bhp per litre
Power to weight 173bhp per tonne
Torque to weight 183lb ft per tonne
Installation Front, longitudinal, four-wheel drive
Construction Aluminium alloy head and block
Bore/stroke 86.0/73.7mm
Valve gear 4 valves per cyl, dohc
Compression ratio 8.5:1
Ignition and fuel Nissan EC ignition, sequential injection, twin Garrett turbochargers with air-cooled intercooler

GEARBOX
Type 6-speed manual by Getrag
Ratios/mph per 1000rpm
1st 3.83/5.6 **2nd** 2.36/9.1
3rd 1.69/12.8 **4th** 1.31/16.4
5th 1.00/21.5 **6th** 0.79/27.3
Final drive ratio 3.55

SUSPENSION
Front Multi-link, coil springs/dampers, anti-roll bar
Rear Multi-link, coil springs/dampers, anti-roll bar

STEERING
Type Rack and pinion, power assisted, Super-HICAS four-wheel steering
Turns lock to lock 2.5

BRAKES
Front 324mm ventilated discs
Rear 300mm ventilated discs
Anti-lock Standard

WHEELS AND TYRES
Wheel size 9Jx18in
Made of Forged alloy
Tyres 245/40 ZR18 Bridgestone RE040
Spare Space saver

NISSAN SKYLINE GTR

VITAL STATISTICS
Body 2dr coupe **Cd** 0.36 **Front/rear tracks** 1480/1480mm **Turning circle** 11.2m **Min/max front leg room** 900/1080mm **Max front head room** 930mm **Min/max rear leg room** 600/780mm **Max rear head room** 850mm **Interior width front/rear** 1430/1395mm **VDA boot volume** n/a **Kerb weight** 1605kg **Weight f/r** 55/45 per cent **Width (inc mirrors)** 1935mm

BRAKES

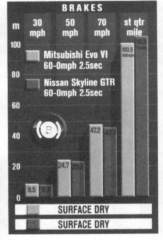

Mitsubishi Evo VI 60-0mph 2.5sec
Nissan Skyline GTR 60-0mph 2.5sec
SURFACE DRY / SURFACE DRY

NOISE
Mitsubishi Evo VI / Nissan Skyline GTR
SURFACE DRY / SURFACE DRY

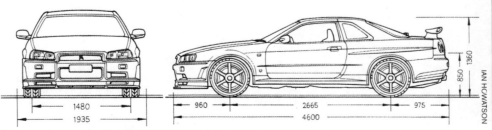

The performance figures were taken at the **Millbrook Proving Ground** with the Evo VI's odometer reading 1150 miles and the Skyline's odometer reading 1200 miles.
AUTOCAR test results are protected by world copyright and may not be reproduced without the editor's written permission

◆ Nissan. But it's not all fake: put your foot down at 40mph in any of the last four gears and the Skyline is left trailing by the wild and wonderful Evo. Which explains why the Mitsubishi fairly demolishes its rival from 30-50mph in fourth (5.0sec versus 5.7sec) and during the 50-70mph run in top (5.8sec versus 11.7sec). The latter is predictable because the Nissan is in sixth whereas the Evo is in fifth, but even if the Skyline driver drops a gear the Evo is still almost a second quicker.

Having said that, there is a slickness and refinement to the Skyline's deceptively muscular performance that, just occasionally, can leave the Evo for dead. Not statistically but subjectively. From its chunkier gearchange to its brawnier engine note, the Skyline always feels the classier performer, even though it isn't quite as quick.

Both cars have brakes that leave you gasping with disbelief the first time you use them in anger. If we prefer the Evo's, it's only because they don't snatch like the GTR's do under light pressure on uneven surfaces.

Evo quicker, but GTR is more cultured
MITSUBISHI ★ ★ ★ ★ ★
NISSAN ★ ★ ★ ★ ★

ECONOMY

It is doubtful whether owners of cars such as these will be terribly concerned about economy, but for what it's worth the Evo is easily the more frugal, averaging 21.2mpg against the Skyline's 18.9. There are several reasons why.

First, it is much lighter than the Skyline: 1365kg as opposed to 1605kg. Second, it has two fewer cylinders and one less turbo with which to devour 98RON unleaded, the preferred diet in both cases. Third, it's so explosive in the mid-range that you don't have to drive it as hard to unleash the same acceleration, which means inevitably the Skyline drinks more fuel when in convoy.

This also provides the Evo with the added benefit of having a longer real-world touring range than the Nissan, despite being fitted with a smaller tank: it will do 250-280 miles, whereas the GTR needs a refill every 200 miles.

Evo less thirsty and has a longer range
MITSUBISHI ★ ★ ★
NISSAN ★ ★

HANDLING & RIDE

One thing's for sure: you'll not find two faster cars than these point to point. Not anywhere, at any price.

Of the two, it is the manic Mitsubishi that is swifter over the ground, just, courtesy of its crazier acceleration and lighter kerb weight, both of which endow it with a level of raw agility that not even the Skyline can level with on twisty roads. But the Skyline counters with a calmer town ride and a wonderful feeling of four-square composure through fast corners. In the end it's a magnificent tussle between two of the finest-handling road cars we're ever likely to sample.

Which says an awful lot about what Nissan has achieved with the new Skyline. Previously you were always aware that you were at the wheel of a big car when driving a Skyline hard. A reduction in unsprung weight through the use of ultra-light wheels and brakes has injected the R34 with a nimbleness and crispness of response that wasn't there before. So much so that you need to dig very deep indeed into the Evo's chassis to put clear air between them.

The tighter the road, the greater the chances that the Skyline will fall behind, true. But here's a thing: even though we all agreed that the Evo was quicker over most ground, we were equally unanimous that the Skyline was more fun. And there are two main reasons why.

Firstly it has much better steering feel than the Evo, whose helm is accurate but strangely numb by comparison. Second, the Nissan's chassis is hugely more adjustable than the Evo's on or around the limit of adhesion.

Ultimately the Evo will do little more than understeer on the road, despite what you may see in the photographs. The Nissan, on the other hand, can be drifted on the throttle like a well-balanced rear-wheel-drive car, and can even be made to power oversteer in the right conditions, lending it a depth of handling vocabulary that is well beyond anything the grippy but understeer-prone Evo can muster.

In terms of sheer mechanical grip, it is the Skyline that hangs on hardest, as you'd expect given the greater size of its bespoke Bridgestone tyres: 245/40 ZR18s all round, as opposed to the Evo's 225/45 ZR17 rubber. But there is a rider to the Skyline's organ-crunching grip: it suffers from tramlining over uneven cambers. The GTR's nose has a tendency to wander over lumpy roads whereas the Evo's doesn't – a small but important price to pay for having such big front tyres and such responsive turn-in.

Evo devastatingly capable, GTR more fun
MITSUBISHI ★ ★ ★ ★ ★
NISSAN ★ ★ ★ ★ ★

Evo is cheaper and more frugal than Skyline, but not as cultured

Use of thin-spoke forged alloys helps reduce unsprung weight

GSR version of Evo has anti-lock brakes, unlike the more focused RS model. But interior lacks quality beside the GTR

R34 interior given a welcome boost by standard-fit Connolly leather-covered seats. Now feels like £50k car

Despite their perceived similarities, these two are very different from each o

HOW THEY COMPARE

	MITSUBISHI EVO VI	NISSAN SKYLINE GTR
PERFORMANCE		
Maximum speeds (mph/rpm)		
6th gear	–	156/5710
5th	150/6900	156/7250
4th	111/7000	131/8000
3rd	81/7000	102/8000
2nd	59/7000	73/8000
1st	41/7000	45/8000
Acceleration from rest (sec)		
0-30mph	1.8	1.8
0-40	2.4	2.5
0-50	3.5	3.5
0-60	4.4	4.6
0-70	5.9	5.7
0-80	7.3	7.4
0-90	9.2	8.9
0-100	11.2	10.8
30-70	4.1	3.9
Standing quarter mile	13.3sec/108mph	13.2sec/111mph
Standing kilometre	24.0sec/134mph	23.1sec/137mph
Acceleration in 3rd/4th/5th/6th (sec)		
10-30mph	5.7/–/–/–	6.0/–/–/–
20-40	4.1/6.6/11.5/–	4.8/6.7/10.0/–
30-50	2.7/5.0/10.0/–	3.6/5.7/8.9/14.3
40-60	2.3/3.5/8.1/–	2.9/4.3/7.7/13.1
50-70	2.5/3.1/5.8/–	2.7/3.7/6.5/11.7
60-80	2.8/3.4/5.3/–	2.8/3.9/5.4/10.4
70-90	–/3.5/5.3/–	3.1/3.9/5.1/9.0
80-100	–/4.2/5.1/–	3.6/3.9/5.5/8.3
Braking: 60-0mph	2.5sec	2.5sec
COSTS		
On-road price	£30,995	£54,000 (est)
Price as tested	£31,940	£54,000 (est)
Interim service	4500 miles	6000 miles
Major service	9000 miles	12,000 miles
Insurance group/quote	20/£1165	20/£1165
Warranty	3 years/unlimited mileage, 3 years anti-corrosion	3 years/60,000 miles, 6 years anti-corrosion
EQUIPMENT		
Automatic transmission	–	–
Airbag driver/pass/side	●/●/–	●/●/–
Anti-lock brakes	●	●
Metallic paint	No-cost option	●
Alloy wheels	●	●
Electric front windows	●	●
Remote locking/alarm	●/●	●/●
Air conditioning	●	●
Front foglights	£385	–
Traction control	–	–
CD changer	Dealer option	●
Leather seats	–	●
HKS sports exhaust	£560	–

● standard – not available

bold type denotes option fitted to test car

SOLD BY	
RalliArt UK Ltd, Kirklands Estate, New Road, Netherton, Dudley DYP 8SY. Tel: 01384 243363	Nissan Motor (GB) Ltd, Denham Way, Maple Cross, Rickmansworth, Herts WD3 2YS. Tel: 01923 899930

COMFORT & EQUIPMENT

Nowhere is the Nissan's lofty price more justified than it is here, in the cabin. The restyled Skyline interior has a look, feel and quality to it that the cheaper Evo interior can't hope to level with.

This strong impression is further enhanced by the Connolly-clad seats that Nissan GB has specified for all 100 R34 GTRs it intends to sell, and by the computer pod that sits on the dash. This provides digital information on everything from turbo boost to fuel injector pressure and is a great source of initial amusement.

For average-shape people the driving position is near-perfect in the Skyline, although taller testers said they'd like to sit an inch lower behind the GTR's adjustable wheel, even with the seat on its lowest setting.

The Evo has similarly dramatic chairs, but unlike the Skyline's they are trimmed in cloth and suede and have a useful extra under-thigh adjustment. If anything they provide even better support than the Nissan's, though they don't look as good.

The Skyline has always been a genuine four-seater, but it has to lose out to the equally roomy Evo on practicality grounds due to the fact that it lacks the rear doors of its rival. The Evo's boot is also a good deal bigger than the Skyline's, which is hard to fathom given the Nissan's greater overall dimensions.

Qualitatively, there is no contest. The Skyline boasts grades of plastic on its dash, door inserts and centre console that make the Evo appear cheap and not especially cheerful inside. Its doors also thunk shut with an oiled precision that makes those of the Evo seem pretty tinny. Even the Nissan's switchgear is now in keeping with that of a luxury car, unlike the previous Skyline's. And the Evo's.

Evo VI has already become a cult classic in the UK, and rightly so at £31k

is mature where Evo is frantic. Ultimately the GTR is the better road car

There are few options that can be specified on either car. Both come with electric front windows, remote central locking, an alarm, twin front airbags and air conditioning as standard. The Skyline goes one better with its standard dashboard computer and its ultra-high-quality stereo with CD autochanger: the latter is listed as a dealer option on the Evo.

But don't forget that the Mitsubishi counters by costing an entire Fiat Coupe 20v Turbo less than the Skyline. So even when fitted with options such as front foglights (£385) and an HKS exhaust (£560), as the test car was, the price is still sensational in this company. Incidentally, fit an HKS exhaust to your Evo VI and it invalidates the warranty, according to supplier RalliArt.

MARKET & FINANCE

Secondhand Skylines do not hold their value especially well, although the fact that Nissan GB has acted as official importer and offered a pukka warranty on the two latest models should mean long term values will improve with time. But of course, the less far you have to fall, the better the landing will be. Which plays right into the hands of the cheaper – yet in many eyes no less desirable – Evo. Both are steep to insure: a 35-year-old with a clean licence is quoted more than £1000 on both. Each is supported by a full three-year factory warranty. The Evo needs more frequent servicing (every 4500 miles), but the GTR's bills are likely to be bigger when they arrive.

GTR is better made, but Evo is roomier	
MITSUBISHI	★ ★ ★ ★
NISSAN	★ ★ ★ ★

Cheaper Evo has to be the better bet	
MITSUBISHI	★ ★ ★ ★
NISSAN	★ ★ ★

Nissan GB will import just 100 GTRs. The first cars go on sale in January

OUR CHOICE

New Skyline is one of the best high-performance cars we've ever driven

HOW THE RIVALS COMPARE			
MAKE/MODEL	LIST PRICE	MPH/0-60	TEST DATE
Audi S4	£37,715	153mph/5.5sec	18.3.98
Competent, quick, but ultimately pretty dull hot version of A4			★ ★ ★
Porsche 911 Carrera 4	£68,000	164mph/4.8sec	9.12.98
The best version of the new 911 outside the hotted-up models			★ ★ ★ ★
Subaru Impreza 22B	£39,950	149mph/5.0sec	9.12.98
Blistering on smooth roads, but not as versatile as Evo VI or GTR			★ ★ ★ ★

What a contest. And what a conclusion. It's always the most dangerous area of our business, comparing cars whose prices are so disparate. But you'll forgive us our sins in this instance, we hope, because all the signs pointed to a head-to-head contest that just had to happen. And that's still how we feel now, after 1000 of the most memorable back-to-back miles any of us can remember.

Yet there is, in the end, no real loser in a showdown like this, despite the fact that everyone involved in the test thought the Skyline to be the superior machine.

The Skyline boasts an aura of completeness, competence and above all desirability that the mad-for-it Evo doesn't even attempt to level with. And in the process it demonstrates perfectly the differences that exist between cars built for competition use and ones that are designed from the outset to be used on the road.

That's not to say the Evo VI is in any way unbearably uncivilised; far from it. However, beside the Skyline it soon becomes obvious that the Evo's motorsport roots are never far from the surface. For some that's a good thing as it endows the Evo with a rawness of appeal that is increasingly missing from many of today's anodised road cars. For others it is merely confirmation of the unusually fine job Nissan has done in making its flagship machine as enjoyable as possible to drive, without going over the edge.

Fact is, these are two of finest enthusiast's cars we've ever encountered, and the knowledge that they both come from Japan should be carefully noted by anyone currently developing a European sports car.

The best one costs the most, but that doesn't mean we think anything less of the Evo VI. If you can afford the Nissan, buy it, comfortable in the knowledge that there isn't a better performance car on the planet that costs less money. If not, stick with the Evo and you won't be disappointed. That much we guarantee.

TEST NOTES

The Skyline's dashtop computer is inevitably the first thing new passengers look towards when they climb aboard. Among other facilities, it allows you to download lap times and telemetry into a PC once you've got the hang of it. But unless you're intending to use the car a lot on circuits, we can't help thinking it's a bit of a gimmick.

Skyline gets even more attention than the Evo on the road, and it's amazing how many people know exactly what it is.

Test Evo VI was exactly the same car that we road tested in March. It's done 12,000 very hard miles since then, but it still felt as good as new. We didn't expect that.

MITSUBISHI	NISSAN
★ ★ ★ ★ ★	★ ★ ★ ★ ★

GTR removes Evo's crown with an amazing blend of punch and polish

REACH FOR THE SKYLINE

NISSAN SKYLINE GTR FINAL REPORT Our everyday supercar has proved as popular with

It's the moment every driver dreads: returning to your car in a multi-storey only to find a gang of youths pacing around your pride and joy and eyeing it covetously. What do you do – shout, run away or call the police? If you own a Nissan Skyline GTR, none of the above. You just engage them in animated discussion about it.

The Skyline is a car for the PlayStation generation, a landmark in late-'90s Japanese

cool. While brothers in arms such as the Subaru Impreza and even the Mitsubishi Evo are an increasingly common sight, the Skyline remains a lesser-spotted rarity. Ours is one of the 100 R33s officially imported by Nissan and handled by Lancashire-based GTR expert Andy Middlehurst, yet despite the growing number of grey imports on our roads, the quirky lines, gaping airdam and adjustable rear wing make it an instant head-turner.

But the great thing, as I discovered in the car park, is that it's the right kind of attention. Teenagers goggle and swoon, enthusiasts stop you to ask about its vital statistics. One guy even took details and contacted me later to tell me he'd bought one. People want to celebrate this thing – and after 20,000 miles I'm still doing just that.

I bought the Skyline for two reasons. Its performance and surefootedness made it a worthy

NISSAN SKYLINE GTR

Car being run for No fixed period
Introduced to the UK 1997
Changes since then New-model R34 with revised turbos and new six-speed gearbox is out now in Japan; here next year
UK sales to date 100 "official" cars
What makes it special The Skyline GTR is a supercar that's useable day in, day out. It offers shattering performance, with driving pleasure enhanced by high-tech four-wheel-drive underpinnings, yet has enough room to seat four and the security of Nissan reliability.

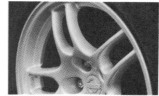

Hairy exhaust; "anti-kerb" tyres

Interior one of few disappointments

the "thinking" four-wheel-drive system, which shifts torque between the axles but crucially lets you enjoy yourself while tidying up after you. The Skyline makes you feel like a hero, but the car's the star.

After the initial adrenalin surge began to wear off I wanted even more. With hindsight, delving into the catalogue of power-boosting add-ons has been a mixed blessing. At its first service, our Skyline gained hotter camshafts and noisy air filters, an exhaust more like an open paint tin than a tailpipe and a tweaked ECU. The result was a power hike from 280 to 400bhp and eye-watering ultimate performance. The flipside, however, was an irritating rasp from the filters and a huge hole at the bottom end. One road tester even

phoned after trying it for the first time to complain something was amiss. At the next service (12,000 miles delayed until 14,272) the power curve was filled in by laptop, but the gains waned after a while.

On the open road, though, the Skyline is simply mighty. Its addictive third and fourth-gear surge quickly persuaded me to fit a radar detector – and to take a keener interest in the location of petrol stations. This isn't a hobby, more a knock-on effect of the car's abysmal touring range. Our mods knocked typical consumption down from 21mpg to nearer 16mpg, but before then I'd taken to wedging a fuel can in the rear strut brace for times when gambling on the last few splashes in the 65-litre tank failed to pay off. ◗

Skyline met heavyweight rivals (right) in our 0-100mph-0 challenge (above)

...ers-by as it has with us, says Simon Daukes

...successor to my recent cars – a Honda NSX, a couple of Porsche 928s and an Audi Quattro – and it promised to mix it with practicality. So far it has more than exceeded the brief.

The driving experience is everything you'd expect from the twin-turbo, four-wheel-drive jobsheet. Performance figures alone don't tell you about what makes the Skyline stand out. Take the fabulous steering, as well-weighted and pure as any power set-up I've sampled, and

R33 has belting performance and clever four-wheel-drive system that helps you out without spoiling all the fun

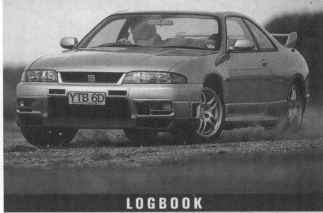

Skyline has demonstrated superb reliability despite its hectic schedule

Carpets tatty after just 3000 miles

The 200-mile gap between fuel stops is an annoying dent in the Skyline's otherwise impressive practicality. To describe it as a two-plus-two fails to do credit to how much room there is in the back, and the boot's pretty sensible, too. Detail items – like fat shoulders on the Bridgestone Potenza tyres which save the rims from kerbing – drive home the point.

The interior is the only other disappointment. The seats are comfy but look like clumsy add-ons, while the trim reminds me of a '70s Cherry in style and quality. Ours needed new carpet in the driver's footwell after 3000 miles because the original had worn away. I can't imagine that happening to many of the Skyline's classier rivals.

Then again, I can't imagine them being such an easy-going blast to own. The Skyline's 60-mile-a-day habit means reliability must feature high up on the agenda, and Middlehurst – who knows it inside out after years of experience with racing and road cars – describes

UK-spec R33s as bomb-proof. We see no reason to challenge this after 20,000 miles. The only blemish was a new clutch friction disc at 14,000 miles, for which a cameo in our 0-100-0 challenge was the culprit.

Having to return the car to Middlehurst's St Helens premises for work complicates matters slightly, but they always pick it up and return it and their service has never been anything less than top notch. At Middlehurst's suggestion we skipped its 1000-mile "running-in" inspection; he also advised that it will run happily on ordinary unleaded rather than super – a relief given its frequent visits to the pumps.

One year on and I'm looking forward to a long and happy ownership, although the biggest threat comes from Nissan itself. After trying the new R34 which hits the UK next year, I'm in love all over again. It does everything mine does, but feels that bit sharper and more tightly screwed together. How long, I wonder, can I resist? ○

We inflicted ugly scratch in bonnet

Hugely enjoyable Nissan can only be replaced by one car – another Skyline

LOGBOOK

TEST STARTED 12.1.99

Mileage at start	100
Mileage now	21,092

MODIFICATIONS

Stage 1 camshafts, replacement ECU, HKS air filters	£2467.50
Performance brake pads	£350

PRICES

List price new	£50,000
Value now	£40,000

FUEL CONSUMPTION

Urban	n/a
Extra-urban	n/a
Combined	n/a
Our test best	24.4mpg

Our test worst	12.2mpg
Our test average	16.5mpg

PERFORMANCE

mph	sec
0-30	1.8
0-40	2.7
0-50	3.9
0-60	5.0
0-70	6.7
0-80	8.2
Top speed	148mph

ACCELERATION IN GEAR

mph	sec
30-50 (4th gear)	8.3
50-70 (5th gear)	11.9

SERVICING AND TYRES

MILEAGE		COST (inc VAT)
6000	Change oil, oil filter, air filter	£293.75
12,000	Change oil, oil filter, air filter, fuel filter	£411.25
18,000	As 6000 miles	£293.75
24,000	As 12,000 miles	£411.25
30,000	As 6000 miles	£293.75
36,000	As 12,000 miles	£411.25
42,000	As 6000 miles	£293.75
48,000	As 12,000 miles	£411.25
54,000	As 6000 miles	£293.75

Labour rate (per hour, including VAT) £58.75
Parts costs Bumper cover £424,18, headlamp £249.10, door mirror £175, windscreen £650.95, wheel without tyre £897.70 (prices include VAT but not fitting)
Tyres 245/4517 RE01 Bridgestone Potenza, £220.38
All figures from Middlehurst Motorsport

FAULTS

3000 miles	Holes worn in carpet on driver's side
12,000 miles	Worn clutch friction disc

COSTS OVER 20,000 MILES

Fuel	£3717.22	Total running costs	£6159.75
Oil (non-service)	None	Running costs	
Service and parts	£1356.88	per mile	29.2p
Tyres	£947.00	Cost per mile including	
Repairs	£138.65 (clutch disc)	depreciation	80.8p

INSURANCE

25-year-old man, single, two speeding fines, five years' no-claims bonus, living in high-risk Manchester (no excess) **£3320.84**

35-year-old man, married, clean licence, five years' no-claims bonus, in low-risk Swindon with garage (no excess) **£807.21**

Quotes from What Car? Insurance (tel 0345 413554); figures based on standard car

WHAT WE LIKE

Simply a fantastic driving experience. Porsche-eating performance and ultra-direct steering, yet reliable and surprisingly practical to run. Feels special even though it's "only" a Nissan.

WHAT WE DON'T LIKE

Appalling touring range because 65-litre tank isn't up to the job. Cheap interior, especially carpet, lets car down. Aftermarket mods have hurt driving pleasure around town.

FINAL VIEW

Everything we wanted it to be: supercar-quick yet useable on a daily basis, durable and roomy with it. Where do we sign up for new R34?

Nissan Skyline GT-R

Tokyo—

The Nissan Skyline GT-R is extraordinary—a muscle-bound, hyper-performance sport coupe that burns rubber with the best Ferraris, Porsches, and BMWs.

The car has been a national cult hero in Japan ever since 1969, when Nissan produced a small six-cylinder sedan called the Skyline GT-R and went racing in Japan with huge success. Ten years ago, the GT-R concept was reborn as a thundering, twin-turbo, four-wheel-drive supercoupe to showcase Nissan's engineering/enthusiast credentials. The car was a sensation. The new GT-R stays true to that philosophy, but the engineers inside the Nissan Technical Center skunkworks have improved the car in every critical area.

Brutal rather than beautiful, the new Skyline GT-R is a car of serious specification and ability. Riding on huge, eighteen-inch wheels, it looks faintly cartoonish from some angles. But drive it, and you soon get past the looks. The GT-R is an immensely fast, very highly developed machine that really connects—something akin to the BMW M coupe, only more so. The GT-R has more space (four seats), more complexity, and a little more weight.

Up front, Nissan worked on the GT-R's old 24-valve 2.6-liter straight-six engine for faster turbo response and more torque. In deference to Japan's Transport Ministry bureaucrats who decree that more than 300 horsepower is sinful, the GT-R's published output is 280 horsepower at 6800 rpm.

For a car that will pulverize the standing quarter-mile in less than thirteen seconds, the GT-R is surprisingly docile in traffic. The engine growls magnificently, and there's a faint turbo background whistle as the revs climb. The real action, however, starts at 3000 rpm, continuing on thereafter like a freight train up to the 8000-rpm redline.

GT-R fans will notice the stronger low- to midrange torque (with 289 pound-feet at the peak), just as they'll appreciate the heavy-duty but precise feel of the new Getrag six-speed manual shifter. With a weighty clutch and solid support from the purpose-designed bucket seat, you begin to get some idea of what the NISMO (Nissan Motorsports) GT-Rs built for the 24 Hours of Le Mans a couple of years ago must have been like.

The biggest single improvement in the new GT-R is body stiffness. Twisting rigidity doubles, and bending strength is up 56 percent. This makes for sharper, more communicative steering, which in turn makes the new GT-R easier to place and trust than its forebears. Turn-in is now fabulous, with the GT-R gripping strongly at the front. And while you might think the combination of variable-torque-split all-wheel drive, four-wheel steering, and sticky 245/40ZR-18 Bridgestones would contrive to kill the fun, that is emphatically not the case. Yippee! The GT-R can still be pushed into playful oversteer slides.

The stiff four-wheel multi-link suspension is not quite perfect, though, for the GT-R's ride is choppy at highway speeds, and on bad surfaces the car can tramline. Still, in a car of this caliber, that's hardly a fatal flaw.

A world away from the Nissans you find running on American roads, the Skyline GT-R is a $42,000-to-$50,000 supercar that's either brilliant or irrelevant, depending on your viewpoint. Would it do wonders for Nissan's image in the United States?

You bet.   —Peter Nunn

the *numbers*

On sale: now (in Japan only)
Price: base $42,000 (in Japan)
Engine: Turbocharged 24-valve DOHC
  6-in-line, 157 cu in (2568 cc)
Power JIS 280 bhp @ 6800 rpm
Torque JIS 289 lb-ft @ 4400 rpm

SKY LARKS

We've lived with our long-term Nissan Skyline R34 GT-R for a month now and it's been truly great fun. Still, we thought we should scientifically quantify how well it goes on road and track. Luckily, it's filled with hi-tech equipment that makes the job a cinch, so we got three testers to drive it in different conditions, then downloaded the data to check out its performance

Words: Richard Meaden-Henderson, Zac Assemakis, Angus Frazer
Photography: Simon Childs, Michael Bailie (track day)

As the first of the three *Top Gear* testers to get their hands on our Skyline, I naturally felt it was my duty to test out its performance on a race track. And, having managed to squeeze in on a track day run by specialists Track Sense at Norfolk's Snetterton circuit (thanks, guys) it was all systems go.

The Nissan Skyline is the only road car to feature on-board telemetry – the kind of readouts that racing drivers rely on to help them improve their track performance. Data is fed back to the driver via a dinky in-car screen, but it can also be downloaded onto a computer in spreadsheet form. This can then be converted into graphs for later analysis – as we've done in the following pages.

It's all a bit technical for me, so luckily I was accompanied by a very trusting, computer-savvy *TG* employee. With him in the passenger seat and a laptop plugged into the car's circuitry, it was time for me to forget the technology and start caning the Skyline round the track. With a 2.6-litre, six-cylinder, twin-turbo 276bhp engine at my disposal, I couldn't wait to get out there.

The 1.952-mile-long Snetterton lap record is 59.475secs, held by a single seater; my best was 87.38secs in a barge of a car. Still, we did many laps and, though I'm no data junkie, I was quite keen to see what's really going on when you're lashing around like a loon.

A flying lap saw us arrive at the first right-hand bend at 119mph in fourth.

Longterm**test**

The revs were spinning at 7,000rpm before I started braking and changing down to third for the first right hander, Riches Corner. As we turned into the 90-degree bend, the speed was down to 66mph, the revs 5,140rpm, and my scare factor was at a peak (although the data didn't record that, of course).

The car turned in beautifully under a constant throttle, but then unexpectedly

twitched mid-bend as, I guess, the rear-wheel steering popped into action and the torque converter moved some of the R-34's 289lb ft to the front wheels.

It was weird and acted very differently from the way a normal rear- or front-wheel-drive car behaves. You can usually feel the oversteer or sense when you're going to run out of grip at the front. But with the Skyline there was no real warning of the jolt and we just had to ride with it. The data showed that, at this point, the torque going to the front tyres was at its highest of all the corners, at 18.8 per cent.

The car settled back immediately and we roared flat-out in third to the next 90-degree right-hander that would lead us onto the back straight. Still in third, the revs peaked at 7,730rpm (which is below the 8,000rpm red line but above the power's 6,800rpm peak), and hit 100mph. As I hit the balance between keeping a decent speed (52mph, as it turned out) and maximum grip, the car's sideways g-force reached over 1g – which is a third of what NASA's astronauts experience at blast off!

The back straight really stretched the Skyline's legs and it felt fantastic. Such

a whopping amount of power let us cover the distance so easily. The torque at the front was quite high as it helped to pull us along, though the majority still pushed from the rear. This is the only place on the track where fifth gear was used – and let it be known that this car still had another gear in hand.

The in-car speedo read 135mph, but the computer's 130mph reading is probably the more accurate of the two. All I know is that I put an awful lot of faith in the Brembo vented discs to haul us down to 57mph in a few hundred feet for the left/right combination of the Esses. Before we flicked through, I dropped from fifth to second gear, our sideways g-force peaked at 1.06g and the Skyline still felt just superb.

Yes, it is a big hunk of a beast, but it's incredibly responsive and very, very keen. You can induce oversteer with the right combination of throttle and steering inputs and, so long as you keep your foot in, it'll straighten itself up with gentlemanly grace. Back on the gas and up to third for the right-handed, slightly-banked Bombhole corner. Any lifting of the gas would unsettle the car's balance and see the

UK's seven-strong Skyline R-34 count reduced to six. Oh, the pressure.

Bombhole saw us hit our maximum of 1.17g. The chassis remained steady throughout, though, and it thrived on a smooth delivery of power and steering. Which is exactly what it got. The gearchanges couldn't be rushed or flat-shifted because this is no tin-pot motor – the lever had a fair way to stretch to engage each gear. Oh, and I had £54,000-worth of car in my hands.

But it didn't stop me raging into the long, fast Coram Curve and provoking 1.05g of sideways force before powering on to almost 100mph and then giving it some heavy-duty braking for the tight, second-gear Russell chicane. The car snaked through the right/left combination with sports-car agility and then it really squatted down on all fours to deliver the goods and unleash its all for the blast up main straight.

After a handful of hot laps the brakes did become spongy, the front tyres started to scuff a little, understeer became a feature and we managed a back-slapping 6.3mpg. Come on!

This is an amazing machine. And the graphs are pretty cool too **VB-H**

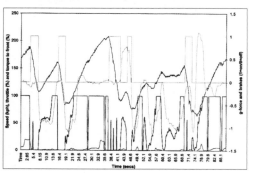

The flying lap starts on the Senna straight. The light-blue line shows the five times Vicki braked on the lap, while the yellow line shows the tum-churning g-forces she pulled (a minus figure is a right turn, a plus is a left)

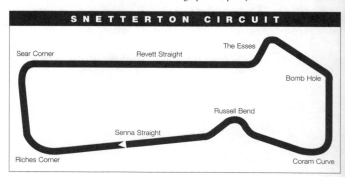

SNETTERTON CIRCUIT

Gutted. Here we have one of the most exciting cars ever to have graced our car park. A car with 276bhp, a ludicrous 0-60mph time and enough electronic trickery to ensure it can take a corner better than David Beckham – and what do we do with it?

Well, Vicki Smutler-Henderson gets to lash around Snetterton in it, Angus gets to drive some amazingly-challenging Welsh B-roads in it, and I get to drive to work. Hey, thanks guys!

Much as I hate to admit it, there is method to this madness. Right from its conception, the Skyline was designed to be a Japanese 911; a supercar that could lap the Nürburgring in record time, but would never balk at the prospect of a rainy and traffic-congested commute. As I've got one of the most appalling commutes in the office, the task has fallen to me to electronically log some of the Skyline's real-world credentials.

In many ways, the Skyline is not a sight you want to see lurking on your drive first thing in the morning. It's a Leviathan that, with the addition of a particularly bright-blue paint job and a giant rear wing, yells 'look at me!' to every other other road user. But that's not what I want from a car at this time in the morning. In fact, all I want to do is pick my nose without an audience and, in an ideal world, I would like to listen to the radio too. That, however, is proving near impossible thanks to the fiddly, over-complicated controls that blight the Nissan's stereo.

About 20 minutes after leaving Hitchin (an apparently-historic market town some 30 miles north of London) I hit the A1(M) and our logging laptop computer beeps into recording action.

Once up to speed on the motorway, I'm flat-lining – well, almost. There's no g, because I'm neither accelerating or decelerating, my foot remains constant on the throttle and the long-legged sixth gear is just fine for keeping the revs low and background noise to a minimum. I might be notching up the miles at a lick, but there's no doubt that motorway driving is like being in a high-speed coma, even in a Skyline.

Aside from the comatose nature of the driving, our Skyline makes a bearable long-distance cruiser. It's an uncompromising car running on ultra-low-profile tyres, so don't expect the comfort levels of a Jaguar XK8, but the jittery ride is borderline, rather than upsetting, while at high speed, the tramlining that blights the car at lower velocities all but disappears.

If the motorway is akin to being in a coma, then when I hit London's congestion, I've died and gone to hell. In fact, looking at the computer analysis, it's a cardiac arrest. Brakes on, brakes off, accelerate, brakes on, off, on, stop. Accelerate – no, brake again. The graph picks up everything apart from the expletives and an average fuel consumption of 16.7mpg. Luckily, the Skyline is mild mannered in town.

Yes, it's bulky, which makes those width restrictions a touch tricky, but there's so much torque you can trickle along in a jam without constantly slipping the clutch, and the spread of power, meanwhile, means I don't have to bother changing gear much either.

Of course, on top of all this the Skyline is a Nissan, so it's less likely to malfunction than a Swiss watch and, come the weekend, you've got the ideal car for a backroad blast – but I'll let Angus tell you about that **ZA**

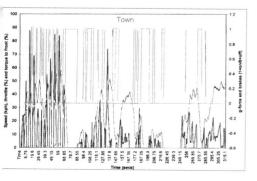

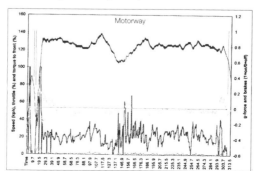

There is a strong contrast between Zac's in-town and motorway graphs – the former is a mountain range of accelerative peaks followed by braking troughs. The motorway is a long smooth plateau with a single brake at each end

- Vehicle Speed (kph)
- Throttle Opening (%)
- Torque to Front Wheels (%)
- Side g-force (g)
- Brake (On:1 Off:0)

 Oh dear. What a shame. Poor old Zac, stuck in a traffic jam, only able to scratch the surface of this car's monstrous reserves of power and fun-potential.

Me, I'm off to some Welsh roads where other traffic is just a rumour. On a purely scientific exercise to see how my data-logging on twisty B-roads compares to Vicki's track heroics and Zac's flat-line commuting, of course.

But gale-force winds, heavy sleet and roads-turned-to-rivers have foiled any attempts I've made at beating Vicki's impressive g-readouts. Damn.

The only half-decent g readings I've logged so far have been when the Skyline had slithered beyond the limits of control. Unless I slow down it's going to be Welsh farmer's Massey Ferguson: 1, *TG*'s Nissan Skyline: 0.

I know that the real aim here is to record and compare the graphs pro-duced by different driving conditions, and returning with an unblemished Skyline should be considered a result, but I'm still determined to have a pop at beating Vicki's g-peaks. And that glowing red sunset promises better weather to come. The only chance is to call the office and beg for an extension.

Amazingly, permission is granted and things begin to look up. It has at last stopped raining and now there's one more 24-hour stint to go Skylining.

Off the mountain and onto wider roads, the pace starts off gently, just to make sure there are no big puddles of standing water for the R34's 17-inch front tyres to aquaplane on. Bumpy B-roads at low speeds aren't the Skyline's greatest strength. It has the off-putting habit of occasionally darting for the hedge on either side, yet when you accelerate, the problem disappears.

According to the Skyline experts at Middlehurst Motorsport, the car's tramlining tendencies are due to the suspension dampers being over-firm. At low speed, the car is relying more on the dampers than the springs. As the speed increases, the suspension is using the springs and the problem goes away. Apparently, softening off the dampers would solve the problem and allow the front to turn in that bit quicker on wet and tight corners.

As it is, though, the R34 feels 99.99 per cent perfect driving south-west from Rhayader to Llandeilo. The roads are still damp, but the Skyline has so much grip you'd never know. And it's *so* fast. You need real restraint or it'll have you at over 120mph far too easily.

It probably isn't the cleverest thing to have your passenger nursing a laptop that records every nanosecond the Skyline strays momentarily above 60mph. Like OJ Simpson leaving a 'My Murder Scrapbook' on the passen-ger seat, things may not go well if we are pulled over by an eagle-eyed officer.

But the Skyline glides through the night and we reach our hotel unhin-dered. Next day, the roads are still wet, but the sky is clear. In these conditions , you'd expect a four-wheel-drive car to be competent and safe, if a bit dull – lots of grip and neutral handling, even-tually giving in to the nose-heaviness of a front-wheel-drive car.

Yesterday, while trying too hard on tighter, rain-sodden roads, the R34 was prone to understeer; here it's prone only to perfection. It may be four-wheel-drive, but the constantly-variable nature of the system means it behaves much more like a rear-wheel-drive car.

Back in our October piece (*TG* 73), that feeling only really came across on the track, not on the dry summer roads. But on wet roads it is much much more pronounced.

You can feel and hear the back end breaking loose out of second- and third-

gear corners. At first it feels a little off-putting, but keep your foot in and the Skyline will get you through with just a whiff of opposite lock. Once the car's in a straight line, it's time for fourth gear. The harder it's worked, the better the six-speed gearbox feels, and the harder it's revved, the better the turbocharged powerplant sounds.

The brakes are excellent too. Have a look at the light-blue line on the graph which, when it's at a peak, illustrates braking. The section of graph covers just over two minutes of driving taken from a five-minute run which was repeated back-to-back four times. I know the brakes faded for Vicki at the track, but on the road they felt as fresh at the end of the day as at the start.

What about Ms Butler-Henderson's maximum g of 1.17; how close did I get to that on the road? Well, I did manage 0.95g swinging into an uphill hairpin. But the best thing about the

bend was that it was just perfect for provoking the R34's tail into drifting out. Get it to lose grip at the rear, keep the power on and you have the handling characteristics of a MkII Group 4 rally Escort – with a bit more bulk.

But the Skyline is on your side. Look how the maximum spike of the yellow g-force line is followed by a peaked green line. The green line illustrates the amount of torque being fed to the

front wheels – 45.5 per cent – to help the car pull itself out of the slide.

At the end of the day, though, I'm also just scratching the surface of the Skyline's mighty abilities. But when I start the trek back to London, boxed in by repmobiles on the M4, I can only conclude that it's better to spend just one day scratching the surface of a Nissan Skyline, than a lifetime plumbing the depths of a Vauxhall Vectra □

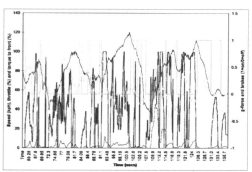

Over a twisty mountain road, Angus's graph is lot more frantic than the smooth racing lines taken by Vicki at Snetterton. After the drive, Angus's electro-cardiograph readings would have looked quite similar to this chart

RED LINE	
Model	two-door coupe
Engine	6cyl, 24v, dohc, twin-turbo
Capacity	2568cc
Max power (bhp @ rpm)	276 @ 6,800
Max torque (lb ft @ rpm)	289 @ 4,400
Transmission	six-speed, 4wd
Suspension	multi-link front and rear
Brakes	vented discs, ABS
Performance	0-60mph in 4.9secs,155mph
Test mpg/combined	16.7/na
Price	£54,000
On sale in the UK	now
Rivals	Mitsubishi Evo VI eXtreme, Porsche 911 GT3, BMW M5

SKY BLUE
We'd buy one because it looks more evil than just about anything else on the road, the handling and performance are superb and it's useable as an everyday car
We wouldn't buy one because the ride is a bit harsh, it tramlines, fuel range isn't great and we couldn't afford the insurance

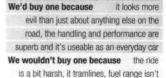

SUSHI QUATTRO

Nissan's seminal Skyline GT-R meets Audi's new RS4 in a high power, hi-tech, four-on-the-floor showdown.
Story by Georg Kacher. Photography by Anton Watts

BEFORE THEIR DNA WAS SO SEVERELY mutated, these were regular family cars. The Audi was an A4 Avant, that up-market German holdall – or at least, overnight bag. For the Skyline, in basic four-door form, think Omega GLS. But then the engineers got carried away, and a bunch of out-of-control chromosomes were spliced in. The resulting machines can still carry you and your brood about, but are also slightly sinister Jekyll-and-Hyde sports cars – equally fast, almost equally entertaining.

At a glance, Nissan and Audi share the same go-faster formula. Take a six-cylinder engine, turbocharge it, mate it to a four-wheel-drive system via a six-speed transmission, add bigger brakes and tyres, bolt on a few spoilers. Then sell the high-performance special for twice the price of the base model. But their characters differ dramatically: they're from different cultures, they pursue different goals.

We drove them back-to-back on the Audi's home turf in Germany, where speed is still a way of life rather than a capital crime. Even so, the road isn't the place truly to savour these philosophical differences. On the race track they come alive and reveal their stories, illustrated by glowing brake discs and smoking tyres. Both drives are memorable, but not always for the same reasons. The GT-R, though its 4x4 system runs awesome computer power, eschews traction control and ESP. Originally, Audi's engineers wanted to go the same puristic way, but then TT syndrome put the frighteners on them and, understandably, they felt compelled to equip the RS4 with ESP as a last-minute safety feature. It hardly ever interferes in the dry and, even when it's off, the handling remains passive because of the inherently even torque split.

The Skyline GT-R isn't about tactics, safety, balance. The Nissan is all about control – your control, not the car's. Pushing hard through the 180 corners of the 12-mile long Nürburgring-Nordschleife, you can hear and sense the four-wheel-drive system as it shifts the action from axle to axle, side to side. This constantly changing torque transfer makes the Nissan feel a little ragged at the edge, until you learn what it's trying to do. Although the Skyline is inherently rear-wheel drive on the entrance to a corner (for better turn-in and steering feel), it modifies itself into a four-wheel-driver on the full-throttle exit. Press on and power oversteer will return through the back door, but it's fast and dramatic enough that you don't really want to stage the subsequent slide on a public road.

The RS4, by comparison, feels unrushed, unruffled. It rolls more, pitches and yaws more, but all its movements are wrapped in cotton wool. Control is also the key mission of the RS4, but it's remote rather than hands-on.

132

'The cars differ dramatically: they're from different cultures, they pursue different goals'

Push the GT-R to the limit, and you'd better be ready to catch the tail with a flick of the wheel. Push the Audi to the same, and you can be ready to answer the phone. This is an amazingly benign car, but it's blindingly quick with it. I haven't had the chance to drive an RS4 in the wet, but on dry tarmac the 380bhp estate simply goes where you point it, and presto. It is virtually impossible to provoke excessive high-speed understeer or oversteer. A four-wheel slide may be on the cards, but it calls for deactivated ESP and a silly entrance speed to your chosen corner.

Straight-line speed is a different matter. On the A92 between Munich and Deggendorf, 155mph can feel almost painfully slow. This autobahn is flat, straight and lightly trafficked. On a sunny day in May, this could be 200mph territory. But not according to Audi or Nissan, who both 'voluntarily' equip their top-of-the-line sportsters with a 155mph governor. The Japanese, masters of self-restraint, even have a 280bhp 'voluntary' power limit. A very special 280bhp, by the looks of it, because the 280bhp Skyline GT-R is marginally heavier than the RS4, and generates more drag. But it's every bit as quick as the 380bhp Audi.

The back roads of Ingolstadt are the playground for the German marque's engineers, and their curiosity is spread evenly between both cars during filling stops

When the Audi engine meets the limiter at 6000rpm in sixth, it's a subtle, gentle interruption. When the Nissan motor cuts out at just over 8000rpm, you hit a wall. The Audi is not exactly super-quiet when you max it, but it's splendid isolation compared to the Skyline, where you're bombarded with industrial noise: turbo whine, tyre roar and slap, driveline hum and the hurricane of passing air, plus zillions of little aural irritations that come and go, come and prevail. Your ears would swear that the GT-R is at least 30mph faster overall. But the speedometer tells the truth, and the truth is a dead heat: top speed is definitely not a factor in this comparison.

REMEMBER, THIS IS AUDI'S BACKYARD AND TWICE A DAY, off the motorway, these idyllic country lanes become the playground for Audi engineers going to and from work. It's an environment where the RS4 and the GT-R do not pass unnoticed. The inevitable questions at the filling station are about appearance and ability. A peek under the Skyline's bonnet instantly silences the batmobile talk. There is a big metallic-red powerplant buried in there, droning and shivering threateningly at idle speed. Grouped around it is the auxiliary equipment which crackles and groans as the heat gets an unexpected chance to dissipate. The struts are linked by a silver bar, which can be adjusted by a pair of giant washers.

The Skyline's business-like underbonnet architecture doesn't hide a tangle of wires and hoses, or a host of stickers in English and Japanese. Pop the lid of the RS4, and be prepared to enter a different world. This is the Hugo Boss of engine bays: tailored, styled throughout, cleaned up, visually and acoustically sophisticated. The arrangement is dominated by a carbonfibre intake plenum carrying the Audi rings and V6 BITURBO message. It's an impressive sight, but clinical all the same. The next RS4 will probably have a sealed bonnet that can only be removed in the shop, like the A2. Modern times…

The Skyline GT-R is like a £999 supermarket computer that has been loaded with expanded memory, ZIP drive, DVD, firewire, all mod cons. It's a fabulous and competent machine, but the basic structure still looks and feels cheap. The doors shut with the bang of a taxi, the dashboard looks like 1965 moulding technology, and the carpets must be a bulk joint purchase with Japan Rail. True, the bucket seats are trimmed in sweet-smelling Connolly hide – done by the UK importer to give it a lift over the grey-import cars – but the padding, the adjustment range and the headroom leave something to be desired. The Skyline forces you into an Italian driving position (stretched arms, legs akimbo), and the pedals are too closely spaced for large feet. The four main instruments are complemented by that famous dash-mounted multi-functional display relaying, to choice; throttle opening, exhaust temperature and the injector opening time – interesting stuff, perhaps, in Tokyo rush-hour traffic, but sheer overkill in the real world. The on-board computer lets you download your personal home-to-work-and-back telemetry, but trying to beat the previous run may lead to a loss of temper, sanity, control, and driving licence.

The cabin of the Audi says Avant rather than RS4. It's an unexpectedly austere station in sombre colours, most of which are a variation of black. Standard equipment includes body-hugging Recaro seats, automatic air-conditioning, a Bose sound system and six airbags. As garnishing inlay trim, the choices are tacky carbonfibre and black piano lacquer, which is much nicer but even… blacker. Like all Audis, the RS4 is available with the useful Navigation Plus system. Beside the stripped-out Skyline GT-R, the 380bhp Avant posits a far sweeter driver environment of comfort, quality materials and failsafe ergonomics, even if it is a much less exciting place to be than the Skyline's all-hell's-going-to-brake-loose-any-minute-now ambience.

Japan and Germany seem to agree that a twin-turbo six-cylinder is a pretty good recipe for the ultimate evolution of a sports saloon, even

The Skyline's twin-turbo in-line six-pot is the same size as the Avant's, but is noisier and more rawly savage. And if it's *really* only 276bhp, we'll eat our hats…

if Audi's is a V6 and Nissan's in-line. Audi fitted the RS4 with a hot version of the five-valve S4 engine, at an identical 2.7 litres, but the cylinder heads have been reworked by Cosworth Technology since it became part of the VW group. Bigger intake and exhaust tracts, more substantial turbochargers and intercoolers, a more ambitious boost pressure and a new free-flow exhaust system helped to increase the maximum power output from 265 to 380bhp at 6100 to 7000rpm. In the process the maximum torque climbed from 289 to 318lb ft, which is available all the way from 2500 to 6000rpm. The RS4 uses the same six-speed transmission as the S4, but it is now spaced more aggressively in third and fourth. The performance is near-magical: the 1620kg estate car will hurl itself to 62mph in 4.9sec. It'll also reach 125mph in 17 seconds – that's to 125mph, note, not 100mph. Fuel economy? Thought you'd never ask. Audi claims an average 23.7mpg, but when you floor it and keep it floored, 14mpg is a more realistic figure. Since the tank holds less than 14 gallons, pit stops are required every 200 miles or so.

The GT-R engine is a direct descendant from the 500bhp-plus GT1 racing unit. In its latest R34 metamorphosis, the 2.6-litre straight six has a pair of smaller, low-inertia turbochargers, a new exhaust with reduced back pressure, a modified lightweight valve train to allow the revs up to the mania of 8000rpm, and stronger con-rod bearings. For political reasons, the maximum stated power output remains an unchanged 280bhp at 6800rpm, but the torque curve is now fuller. It peaks at 4400rpm, where 289lb ft are on tap. Mated to a six-speed Getrag gearbox, it pushes 1540kg of Skyline to 62mph in 5.2 sec. The top speed is a self-restrained 155mph, but the claimed fuel consumption is an unrestrained 20.3mpg, and when the road is clear this car, too, will happily dwell on the wrong side of 14mpg. The pronounced thirst isn't only down to the driver's right hoof, but also the drag of both cars. All those panels, wings and deflectors are aimed more at reducing lift and getting cooling air to engines and brakes

than cutting drag. Against any other A4, even the S4, the RS4 has lowered suspension, bespoke springs and dampers, and a quicker steering rack. Besides, much of its four-link front axle is replaced by aluminium components. The nine-spoke cast-alloy wheels are shod with 255/35ZR 18 tyres. Offering a limited variation in torque split between the axles – from 25:75 to 75:25 – the quattro 4wd system is supported by ESP, EBV (electronic brake force distribution), ASR (traction control), EDS (electronic diff lock) and MSR (drive-by-wire throttle).

But specification is no substitute for quick reflexes, and the RS4's reactions are slowed down by the indifference built into some of the controls. Take, for instance, the massive ventilated disc brakes. Obviously nothing less than colossal power would do, and you get it, but they're handicapped by mushy pedal feel. An attempt at a quick gearshift is thwarted by a gearlever that seems to relay shift orders to the transmission via rubber bands. Dab the throttle, and hang on, what's this… a generous dose of old-fashioned turbo lag. Turn the steering wheel, and experience the same pothole kickback, the same momentary dethrottle slack and the same full-power tug that all other A4s display, but in a more pronounced fashion. Don't get me wrong: these flaws don't impair the Audi's ground-covering ability, especially when it rains. But they take away the cutting edge. Is Audi sacrificing the Sunday morning drive to build an all-week car? Or could it have done both?

The Skyline has a state-of-the-art, on-demand four-wheel-drive system. As soon as sensors signal a loss of rear grip, up to 50 percent of the available torque will be directed within one-hundredth of a second to the front wheels. Since the initial oversteer almost automatically corrects itself, you need to keep your right foot planted to encourage a powerslide that can last a long way through and out of the bend. Unlike the brake and throttle-linked ESP preferred by Audi, the GT-R relies on a complex rear-wheel-steer system to counteract

A far superior driving environment which delivers awesomely competent power with little fuss and no bother. But is RS4 a little *too* grown-up against the Skyline?

excessive yaw, understeer and oversteer. It also employs an active limited-slip differential to improve the cornering grip, a set-up which often reacts in a sudden, unsubtle manner. Instead of putting an electronic buffer between car and driver, the Nissan serves up a sudden breakaway. It's a characteristic supported by the uncompromising 245/40ZR18 Bridgestone Potenza RE040 tyres which tend to break away much more suddenly than the Audi's pleasantly creamy new-generation Pirelli P Zeros.

What makes the Skyline really special is the way it responds. This car translates driver inputs one-to-one, without adding or altering, without delay or distortion, and without making decisions before they are due. The clutch is light and sharp and progressive. The six-speed gearbox is a two-finger affair that combines short throws with total precision. The Brembo brakes are instant-on, and they never seem to wilt, not even after five consecutive hot laps on the Ring. The throttle dives deep into the footwell and is a joy to modulate, with effort and response striking a perfect balance. The steering is surprisingly light and always alive, supplying an accurate blueprint of the road and the car's reaction to it. At 2.5 turns from lock to lock, it is also quick enough to give you a head start against the law of physics.

Sounds like perfection. Isn't quite that, though. The official Nissan import car is built to track-friendly V-Spec, which means very hard suspension, a tiresome tendency to tramline, and a ride that's borderline unacceptable, not just because of comfort but because it can let the car get lumped and bounced about on poorly surfaced roads. Sometimes, when it's narrow too, it feels like you've simply got too much Skyline.

FIVE EYES WOULD BE USEFUL HERE. KEEPING ONE EYE (at least) on the road ahead is a permanent must, but then there's another needed to scans the horizon for trucks and Dutch tourists, one for the mirrors, one to glance at the instruments, and one on a constant lookout for the law. Ordinary humans who can only spare two eyes at a time will find the Audi a much easier car to live with. It is less edgy in its actions and reactions, more forgiving all the way to the brink, not as challenging when the going gets tough.

While the GT-R aims at amateur racers who don't mind getting up at 6am of a Sunday to blast up and down their favourite country road, the RS4 targets people who are always under time pressure, maybe ultimately less interested in the going than in the getting there. Nine out of 10 drivers will find the car from Ingolstadt a more confidence-inspiring vehicle, and it won't take long to get used to. It is competent, comfortable, capable and very quick on all surfaces and in all weathers, but its remarkable ground-covering ability is blurred by a suspicion of dullness.

Crunch time. If a single day's driving was the decider, the Nissan would win hands down. It is clearly the more involving car, the bigger challenge, the more entertaining man-machine interface. But one day doesn't tell the full story. What is the verdict after a week, a year? Would you still tolerate the boy-racer livery, the deafening noise pattern, the cramped cabin? I'm sure I would – but only if the GT-R was not my only car. This is a great plaything when the time is right and the conditions are right. As a daily driver, however, I'd readily trade some of the Nissan's excitement for the finesse and the all-round ability of the RS4. While it may do less for your glands, the Audi smooths the adrenalin flow by being a lot smoother without losing speed. It is also more forgiving, more practical, more comfortable and less expensive. And its feels like part of a lovingly made object. The Skyline puts the craft deeper under its skin.

Ingolstadt is sending 400 RS4s to the UK, all of which – £46,500 price tag notwithstanding – are pre-sold. That's against the limited local supply of 90 £54,000 GT-Rs, half of which are still available. The Avant is the more sensible choice, the Nissan the more rewarding drive. Take your pick – for a change, you can't go wrong.

used **car** guide

Photography Simon Childs Details Derek Goard

SKYLINE **R33 GTR**

A mighty machine that still posseses enough decorum to placate your dear old grandmother

A hi-tech tour de force, brutal grunt with brutish looks, an everyday supercar; Nissan's Skyline is all of that and more – an awe-inspiring mix of computer brains and straight-six brawn.

If you haven't got the necessary £54k for the latest incarnation, the R34 GTR, how about its forebear, the R33? Launched in '95 in Japan and sold until early '99, it has slightly softer looks and a bit more cabin room. You may not get all the R34's cutting-edge toys, but you'll still have a 2.6-litre, 276bhp twin-turbo, plus computer-controlled all-wheel drive with four-wheel steering. And with 60mph arriving in just 5.4secs, you won't miss out on any thrills.

CHOOSING

The R33 came in more flavours than just the GTR – but that's the one to pick. A rare two-litre, non-turbo GT is a Skyline in name but little else, while the 2.5-litre single-turbo GTS still lacks the 4WD technology and beefier

looks of the GTR – compare an RS2000 with an Escort Cossie and you get the idea.

So stick with the GTR. While the 'base' model offers a limited-slip diff, the V-Spec version has lower, stiffer suspension and an active viscous limited-slip diff. The latter mostly shows its advantage on a track rather than the road, has a harder ride and costs about £1,500 more from a dealer, so consider if you really need one.

With just 100 official UK R33 GTRs sold (November '97-on), you may have trouble finding a British market car. Note that UK cars are *all* V-Spec and have an extra oil-cooling kit.

So, you're more likely to come across a grey import from Japan – at least 75 per cent of UK cars will be greys. Although not all Japanese Skylines will be bad bets, there is the issue of verifying a grey's pedigree. Spend £25k without being able to check on a car's past and you'd be very brave and/or very daft. A verifiable history is vital in proving proper care (turbos need

regular servicing), so the best greys are cars imported new and serviced in the UK. For this reason, we'd shy away from anything that's lived in Japan. If you do go for one, the longer a car has lived in Britain the better.

Skylines are often the target of the tuner's art, but, for peace of mind, pick the most standard car you can find – particularly if you aren't up to speed on tuned cars and driving them. Most work is done properly, but you still want the safest bet you can, and there's the question of how a tweaked car may have been driven.

Signs of tuned motors include stickers (or their remaining sticky patches), extra gauges, aftermarket carpets with names like Nismo (Nissan's tuning bods) or very obvious engine work. Air filters and sports exhausts are often the first things to be done and may indicate further modifications to the car.

If the engine's been tuned, remember the rest of the car may need bolstering to cope – R33s

Do it right and there's the potential to storm to 60mph in just 5.4 seconds – and that's in a regular Skyline R33

Check that the gearbox (especially the synchro on fourth gear) hasn't suffered due to abuse – it shouldn't go 'crunch'

Aim for a standard-tune car if you can. If it has been modified, speak to the people who did the work on it

Smoking or howling turbos are a no-no, and bear in mind that cars running over one bar of boost need steel turbos

The R33 is a proper four-seater, with more cabin space than the R34 version, although its boot is a bit smaller

Brakes and alloys can be very expensive – so if they need replacing allow for these costs when you're haggling

Clever four-wheel-drive technology and four-wheel steering give the car amazing abilities; it's easy day-to-day too

Clocking is a danger, especially on imports with no history. Be wary of a car looking old before its time

You want as much checkable history as you can get – a UK FSH and all the old invoices are the ideal documents

As clever as a Skyline's computers may be, it's still not impossible to stuff one – so watch out for crash damage

INFO

BUY

UK cars are the safest bets (but can cost **10-20** per cent more than greys). Grey **imports** that have spent **all** their life here. A **verifiable UK** service history is a must-have. Only go for **V-Spec** option if you really need it.

AVOID

GT and **GTS** models. A just-imported, tuned-up grey with **no papers** – unless you're very **brave**. **Tatty** cars may have had negligent owners. **White** cars are the least desirable and worth **less**.

COST

95M R33 GTR	
34k miles	£18,000
95M R33 GTR	
14k miles	£26,250
96N R33 GTR V-Spec	
15k miles	£25,000
96P R33 GTR V-Spec	
24k miles	£23,000
97P R33 GTR V-Spec	
11k miles	£29,000
98S R33 GTR UK V-Spec	
7k miles	36,000

PARTS

Main dealer (Middlehurst Nissan) prices for an R33 GTR V-Spec, including VAT

Brake discs (pr)	£642.73
Brake pads (set)	£300.80
Clutch	£352.50
Wheel bearing:	
Front	£35.25
Rear	£123.38
Starter (p/ex)	£272.60
Front bumper	
cover	£306.68
Alloy wheel	£897.70

SERVICE

Prices from Middlehurst Nissan, including VAT

Every 6k miles/6mths	
Minor	£235.00
Major	£352.50
Cambelt service	
(48k/4yrs)	£277.30

INS GRP

All	(20)

CLUB

UK Skyline GTR Register Tel: 01293 851944 http://www.gtr.co.uk

running more than 1.1 bar of boost should be on steel turbos instead of the ceramic ones, for example. Again, it all comes to checkability – if a car has been under the knife, ensure there are invoices to back up the work, and speak to the surgeons in question. If it's been tuned in Japan, not only will this be a lot harder – making a modified, just-in-from-Osaka grey import our least encouraged buy of all – we recommend a gentle trip straight to a Skyline tuning specialist to ensure it'll run properly here and not need Japanese 100 RON fuel and the like.

Money-wise, you get what you pay for, and it'd probably be tricky to find a good, low-miles private car under £20k. Dealers start about £25k and go up to around £35k for latest R33s. UK cars cost 10-20 per cent more than greys too.

PROBLEMS

It's a specialist buy, so get an inspection before doing so – preferably by someone who knows

their Skylines. But before you call in help, you can still whittle down the contenders yourself.

Use the service history to speak to everyone who has owned and worked on the car, not least to be on guard against clocking. If it's a grey run abroad, you're at a disadvantage – a certificate of mileage on the mph speedo conversion is a boon, but not all will have one. See if the tyres, pedals, etc seem over-worn for the age, though without mats, carpets will be pretty worn by 20k miles anyway. Incidentally, a 'Middlehurst history' refers to Nissan's only UK Skyline main dealer, based in St Helens.

Skylines generally hold up to the job well, but abuse may have led to gearbox maladies, particularly the third/fourth gear synchro. Ensure that it engages without graunching, otherwise it could be a £700-1,000 bill to fix. Ask what boost the turbos are running on (0.7 bar is standard) and be wary of any smoking or howling. Watch for low oil pressure too,

as such woes could cost you £2-3k. Pinking engines won't last too long, and this may be a result of too much boost on tuned cars, the wrong octane fuel or incorrect ignition timing.

A clutch that only bites at the top of its travel could well be on the way out, and if the car has a racing clutch, consider what it's been up to.

Alloys are massively expensive, so check they're not damaged, and peer through at the brake discs' rims – wear more than 1mm deep means they'll need skimming or replacing. Official Nissan brakes are painfully pricey, but you can get higher-spec ones for less money.

If it's meant to be a V-Spec, get under and ensure the rear diff has cooling fins on it to be sure. Watch for stone chips, worn tyres, envy scratches, a grounded-out front spoiler, etc. And always be on guard for bad crash repairs – check the engine bay, examine shut lines and inspect paint finish. Then, when you're happy with that, get a pro to do it all again □

COOGAN'S RUNABOUT

Much has been said about the thrill of driving the Nissan Skyline GT-R. Nothing has been said about what it's like to live with one. Until now

**Story by Steve Coogan
Photography by Jason Furnari**

ONE OF THE MANY PERKS OF BEING A MINO celebrity, along with film premiere invites, shampe adverts, fawning magazine profiles and the priority aisle detox farms, is getting the opportunity to drive cars mo capable than I am. As a comic writer/performer, explorin the outer limits of serious automotive hardware is n within my remit. I'll never know just what a serious c can do. But as a minor celebrity, I can still have one f free, so I drive it anyway.

And that's exactly what has happened with the Niss. Skyline GT-R, or Godzilla, as it is affectionately referr to by its followers. (Is it possible to liken anyone to a sca tower-tall fire-breathing lizard with any skerrick affection? 'C'mere, you appalling monstrosity, you.' have not the slightest pretension toward being ab to master a 280bhp twin-turbo, 155mph car, but I' always wanted to have a go in one. And that's all it tak For me, anyway.

So I've got an R34 GT-R V-spec for a few months, a it's my duty to tell you what it's like as an ownersh proposition. Living with a Skyline: the highs, the lov the curious semaphore I'd get from motorcycle couri whenever they saw me in it, where they appeared to miming shaking a glass of water.

Now, my initial view of the Skyline – never call i Nissan, or people will think you drive a Micra or a mir cab – was that it seemed like one of those deep-sea dive watches fashionable in the '70s. They'd stay intact to depth of 250 metres, long after your lungs had collapse Which was very impressive, but relatively pointless wh you were dead and the Krakens and giant squid had been reading the right fashion supplements. Not alt gether pointless, however, because there is a relevan

concerning potential and appeal to people in the know. And should you yourself get the chance to step inside one and take a spin, this notion is backed by what actually happens in the street. It makes you self-conscious, incredibly aware of what it is you're inhabiting. Each car should be issued with a cast-iron ego in a presentation box.

Because whenever I drive it past a couple on the street, the guy turns and points in a 'do you know what that is' kind of way. The girl shrugs in a 'that's a vulgar penile compensator with a coffee table nailed to the boot' kind of way. Petrolheads and car enthusiasts know that this is a near-mythical Japanese beast tamed by an updated version of HAL from *2001: A Space Odyssey* lurking inside. But I'm not sure that they are the sort of people I'd like acknowledgement from.

And on that technology, I namechecked HAL for a reason. Because what's going on in there, the level of artificial but somehow organic intelligence and competence, is equally impressive and intimidating. Sometimes I swear I could hear a voice saying: 'Attention, Steve, you've approached that bend too fast and it's wet, you're getting it all out of shape, do you want me to sort it out for you?' And before waiting for an answer, does so anyway. The Skyline commands a kind of respect – for the driver, the sort you might have for a drill sergeant, and for certain observers the kind they'd never admit and disguise under a thick veneer of lofty scorn. It's

a little like the policemen at Heathrow airport armed with sub-machine guns: potentially lethal but unlikely ever to be called upon to fire and consequently a bit awkward. Regardless, whenever I make eye contact with those airport guys, I nod and smile politely as if to say: 'You'll get no trouble from me, officers. I am not a terrorist.' And that's what other drivers do to me when I'm behind the wheel of the Skyline. A penile compensator, sure. But the *thinking* man's penile compensator.

Aesthetically, I haven't made my mind up. I actually prefer the shape of the previous R33 GT-R. It looked like a bouncer in a shellsuit. Electric metallic blue on the outside with a cherry red interior is just a bit too much. Maybe if the body was silver or the seats black the effect wouldn't be so retina-searing; if it were brash on the outside, quiet on the inside or vice versa. This is loud on the outside, and cacophonous on the inside; a wolf in Superwolf's ('Ta daaaa') clothing.

The brushed aluminium-look interior (actually plastic) looks good but feels cheap to the index-finger-knuckle-knock test. The leather seats grip you all over in a way probably beloved by Tory backbenchers and other hide fetishists, but not entirely relaxing. Then again, the Skyline is not really an elbow-out-the-window, ooze cruise kind of experience. You need both hands on the wheel to counter the bump steer, for one thing. The wheel is alive, like a snake encircling the Momo spokes,

'I swear I could hear a voice saying: "Steve, you're getting it all out of shape. Do you want me to sort it out for you?"'

Skyline is capable of turning the most sensible adult into a kid again. High level of driver involvement is addictive but can get too much

wriggling and jiggling constantly, recording road surface impressions like a record needle. If there's a paper clip on the road you get to know about it (why didn't Ferrari give the F355 steering like this?).

And very dominant in the forward view is that electronic display screen, squatting atop the facia and drawing the gaze of frustrated fighter pilots, a bit like the telemetry display screen you see straddling F1 cars, and which Coulthard and Co gaze at intently. Irvine's checking to see if there's a porn channel. Probably.

In fact, it's more than a bit like it. It's almost exactly like it. Everything about your car – boost pressure, intake temperature, driving seat methane content under cornering – is available for inspection. And anyone who seriously suggests any of the information displayed is at all useful needs to get (a) out more or (b) a girlfriend. Sat-nav would have been more useful. But it is a laugh, flipping from mode to mode and saying to your passenger in a solemn Dr Spock fashion that lift-off is imminent. Which would be entirely likely without that coffee table. There's even a g-force indicator to tell you what your internal organs are already broadcasting: you've stopped suddenly, gone round a corner quickly or are accelerating rapidly. Just in case the fact that your cheek is squashed up against the driver's window and your skeleton is threatening to emerge from your skin wasn't a big enough clue. What all this does do, though – the gripping seats, the driving position and the computer display – is issue a major wake-up call on precisely what it is you've strapped yourself into.

But now a real bonnet bee for me: why do serious driver's cars have the most fiddly music systems? I had to pull over to select a station or change the tone/balance *et al*. Maybe that's the idea; diverting your attention from controlling the beast to dial up your favourite Johnny Hates Jazz number is potentially bad for your health. But to high-performance car manufacturers I would say that you need bigger buttons when you're driving quickly. Volvo does it properly; why can't anyone else?

But enough whingeing. The wheels look fantastic in that brake-dust-metallic grey and the gold calipers are a reassuring reminder that this car stops as well as it goes.

And oh, does it go. The boys at *CAR* left me some appetising blurb in the glovebox when I first picked it up. 'Enjoy the car,' it said. 'Everything you've read about it is true.'

The ride is track-car hard. I have scheduled an appointment with my orthodontist for the day I hand it back. It and the steering are so chatty that if you're paying attention, you almost don't need dials and displays to assess information. Just your fingertips, inner ear and seat of your pants. It enables you to drive at speed with total confidence.

Build quality, too, is amazing, I could hear nothing rattling above the noise of my colliding bones. Overall, there is a developed-by-the-military feel. You don't see GT-Rs that often, which adds to the put-together-in-a-bunker-deep-in-the-Rockies impression. Drive it and another layer of sensation comes across: overwhelming competence done with style. The car is Arnold Schwarzenegger and Jean-Claude Van

'The electronic display screen says to your passenger in a solemn Dr Spock fashion that lift-off is imminent'

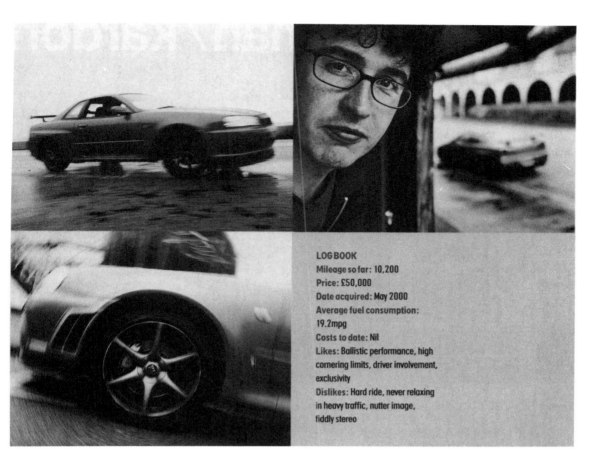

LOG BOOK
Mileage so far: 10,200
Price: £50,000
Date acquired: May 2000
Average fuel consumption:
19.2mpg
Costs to date: Nil
Likes: Ballistic performance, high
cornering limits, driver involvement,
exclusivity
Dislikes: Hard ride, never relaxing
in heavy traffic, nutter image,
fiddly stereo

Damme crossed with Nadia Komanechi and Dame Margot Fonteine. A pay-per-view prospect, I think you'll agree, but you know what I'm trying to say: it's a combination of brute strength and finesse, power and élan.

There's a bit of turbo lag below 3000rpm, but it makes the warp factor speed all the more dramatic when it kicks in. It's like nitrous bloody oxide. The car goes very fast for a long time, and then it, well, it just goes faster. But you don't need to go fast for people to move out of your way. In their rear-view mirrors, an R34 hunching its way onwards makes it look like a machine-gun bunker is gaining on them.

Okay, straight-line speed on a dry day is something you'll find in any piece of exotica. Even a V6 Toyota Camry goes quickly when you floor it, for Heaven's sake. But what makes the Skyline different, provides some meat as filling – and adhesive – between superlatives, is the way it corners in the wet. Witness: I went around a slow corner and booted out the back end. Now, in a Ferrari or Porsche, the unskilled would back off and traction control would step in and tidy things up for you. Or guide you gently backwards into a wall if the control is off.

But in the Skyline, you can keep your foot planted into any corner with impunity, and the various electronics will take care of your tomfoolery and sling you away in the direction that you wanted to go. You can sense the currents of information and reaction bouncing around underneath you, like a pinball ricocheting from bell to stop, as they transfer with the current of power between all four wheels, depending on where it's needed most. There are bends where the car scoots around the corner, but my subconscious makes a puncture mark in a hedge and is sitting, bewildered, in a field. Quite astounding.

To enjoy the Skyline, to really get the most out of it – by which I mean the extremely humble portion of its massive abilities you're ever likely to access – you have to either put it on a track or drive like a nutter. I don't want to do either. I enjoy taking in the view while I'm driving, and if you look out of the window of a Skyline, unless it happens to be the windscreen, then you might end up upside down in that self same green pleasantry.

Alas, real-world driving means bumper to bumper on the M25, in which case I want to look at a bit of wood and leather (not a Rover, thanks) and listen to Burt Bacharach. At those times I'd rather have a Jag. A Skyline is no place for Burt, unless it is the car that his kidnappers have used as a getaway vehicle and he is trussed and gagged in the boot. Maybe it is impending middle age that prompts me to make observations of the 'boy racer's wet dream' variety about this car. It certainly should not be in the hands of anyone over 40. Imagine someone in that age bracket – say, Frank Dobson – driving one. He might as well have bleached blond hair and a skateboard under his arm. In fact… no. But at least the beard would have looked in place. And he certainly could have moved to Brighton. There's plenty of guys like that there.

If Aston Martin could pack the electronic guts and entrails of the Skyline into the DB7's sexy body, I might well think again. So far we've had a nice, left-breathless-with-pink-cheeks fling, but it doesn't look like we'll be getting married.

> 'The car scoots around the corner, but my subconscious makes a hole in the hedge and is sitting, bewildered, in a field'

⬤ NISSAN Skyline GT-R M-spec

This is the final evolution of the R34 Skyline before an all-new model arrives in 2003, and it's rather good...

Any GT-R diehard knows that Nissan built the original R-32 Skyline GT-R back in 1989 for one reason. To win races. And it did, not only in Japan, but also in Australia where its 4wd, twin-turbo, hi-tech wizardry blitzed the touring car championships for two straight years.

The man who was to become known as 'Mr GT-R', Kozo Watanabe, followed that racing tradition with the R-33 and R-34 models into the nineties including specially tuned V-spec variants.

Then, as if to signal the radical change of direction that chief exec Carlos Ghosn had chosen for Nissan, Watanabe was gone from the picture, replaced by a new team of engineers headed by Kazutoshi Mizuno, former Nissan Le Mans chief engineer and Group C team manager.

And one of the first things Mizuno did, while he and his team worked on the handling traits of the new V35 Skyline saloon, was to modify the GT-R's V-spec suspension set-up. He felt that its harsh, highly strung, razor-edged road-handling characteristics were good for circuit racing – on smooth racetracks – but that in the real world, on real roads, it needed more compliance. The resulting M-spec (obviously using the M from Mizuno!), is not just a better rounded GT-R on all road surfaces, but has repercussions for the sportscar on a worldwide scale. More on that in a minute.

A quick spin around the mountains south of Tokyo was enough to see what Nissan has achieved with its latest, and final incarnation of the R34 GT-R.

Like the new V35 Skyline saloon, the M-spec employs Nissan's new 'ripple-control' shock absorbers which work to soak up even the smallest bumps or road undulations to maximise tyre contact with the road. To further ensure

the rear stays planted, Mizuno also fitted a modified rear anti-roll bar and revised all the spring rates to enhance the effect of the ripple control upgrade. Whether at high speed on a highway or at lower speeds on the twisty bits, the new suspension set-up is where the R-34 should have started. Not only does it provide a more supple ride. It also allows an average driver more leeway when cornering hard, as you don't have to worry about the tail stepping out so far and so fast. When it does start to go, it is easier to catch and control.

'Of course the M-spec offers a far more comfortable ride on public roads and highways, but its race heritage has not been ignored,' said Mizuno. 'I would say the M-spec is more suited to endurance races while the V-spec is better suited to short sprints where hundredths of a second mean everything.'

But the bottom line is that the M-spec is the future for the GT-R. It gives us a glimpse of where Nissan is going to take its next generation sports flagship.

Retuned suspension has given the GT-R the more supple suspension it was crying out for

Ghosn has made it quite clear that he wants future GT-Rs to be a showcase of Nissan's top-end technology in the US and Europe (alas there are no plans by Nissan UK to officially import this car).

To that end, the GT-R must employ a suspension system that does not jump and bounce around on marginalised surfaces but one that can handle the high-speed touring on the autobahns and autostradas of Europe. One Nissan source said that during a test at 250kph on the autobahn, 'the V-spec's harsh settings led to temporary traction loss as the car jumped all over the place'. Mizuno's modifications give it the capability to cruise effortlessly at that speed and higher – essential if it's to compete with the Porsche 911.

It is common knowledge that the next generation of Japanese sports cars, including the new NSX, GT-R and a strongly rumoured V8-powered Toyota

4300GT, will all pack 400bhp-plus, thus placing them head to head with the likes of the Porsche 911 Turbo, Ferrari 360 and BMW M3. It soon becomes clear that the benchmark for the M-spec's handling was Porsche. A comparison test with a 3.4-litre Carrera 4 showed that the ride and compliance of both are closer than they've ever been before. And when it comes to traction and roadholding over seriously testing roads, the revised GT-R can teach the 911 some tricks.

Driven back to back over the same stretch of winding mountain road, the Porsche's limits of adhesion were reached long before we dared take the M-spec any further. At around 60mph on one long uphill left-hander, a minor mid-corner undulation threw the 4wd Carrera's rear up and outwards, requiring armfuls of opposite lock to correct it. Travelling at least 5mph faster, the M-spec took that same mid-corner bump in its stride, displaying adhesion limits that no European rival could compete with.

Another aspect of the M-spec that helps makes it the most desirable GT-R ever, is the attention to detail inside and out. Finished in a new gold silica paint, the car's surface colours change depending on the angle with which light reflects off it. And inside, Nissan offers some rare craftsmanship. Back at the factory, a couple of leather workers have been specially employed to cut top quality leather for the M-spec's moulded bucket seats with stitched GT-R emblem, steering wheel, gear shift and hand brake lever. This takes time, which is limiting production to 50 cars a month.

Now imagine the 2003 model GT-R with its expected 400bhp and the M-spec's more compliant suspension and classier interior, and you'll see that this car is the missing link to the next generation of Japanese supercars. Can't wait!

Peter Lyon

SPECIFICATION	
Engine	In-line 6-cyl, 2568cc, twin turbo
Max power	276bhp @ 7000rpm
Max torque	289lb ft @ 4400rpm
Top speed	165mph (claimed)
0-60mph	4.8secs (est)
Price	5.95 million yen (no UK price)
On sale	Now (in Japan)

evo RATING	★★★★1/2
⊕ Chassis tweaks make the GT-R great again	
⊖ You'll have to import one yourself	

Photography: Hiroshi Kodaira

'When it comes to traction and roadholding
over seriously testing roads, the revised
GT-R can teach the 911 some new tricks'

abin has a more upmarket feel, thanks to the fine hides that now cover the bucket seats, wheel, etc. Twin turbo straight-six is unchanged, though quoted 276bhp feels more conservative than ever...

SETTING SONS

The R34 Skyline dies in August and with it goes the familiar straight-six and chiselled shape. David Yu savours three generations of boxy but brilliant Skyline GT-Rs

ontrary to popular belief, I wasn't the first to coin the name 'Godzilla' to describe a Skyline (some of you will remember my tuned, 620bhp R33 GT-R that used to terrorise these pages). In fact the 'Godzilla' moniker was first used by awe-struck Aussies who watched their beloved Holdens get eaten alive by fire-breathing R32 Skyline GT-R Group A race-cars in their domestic touring car championship back in 1990.

That was my first exposure to the Skyline legend too, and when the opportunity came up later that year to try an R32, I was dumbstruck by its ability, but decided I would probably kill myself trying to find its limits. Five years later, of course, I found myself driving up the M6 in a friend's F355 to pick up a tuned 440bhp R32…

But let's forget tuning for a moment and assume you had the choice between a standard R32, 33 or 34. Which is the most capable, which is the fastest and which is the most fun?

Luckily for **evo**, I founded the Skyline GT-R Register (UK) back in '95 and a request on their very active web forum (www.gtr.co.uk) quickly yielded a suitable example of each generation. This was actually less likely than it sounds since well over 90 per cent of the Skyline GT-Rs in this country have been tuned to some extent.

Dave Redpath's 1989 R32 is one of the first built, but has done just 50,000 miles and had two previous owners, one in Japan and one in New Zealand. The latter loved the car enough to bring it with him when he moved to the UK. Finished in unprepossessing gunmetal grey, his car is standard apart from a subtle Trust exhaust.

Although you couldn't call it elegant, the R32 does have a pleasing simplicity to its aggression. The flared arches look subtle in comparison to its successors' and the rear spoiler is almost dainty. The design has aged very well and yet, due to its relative rarity, it is the least likely to attract unwanted attention from cops or robbers.

The interior features one of the best driving positions there is, with comfortable, supportive seats, pedals perfectly positioned for heel-and-toeing and a chunky, precise but non-rushable gearchange. The shapely leather steering wheel at first feels a tad large compared with some more modern machinery, but soon feels natural. The only dated aspect is the pod-mounted windscreen wiper control that unfortunately required plenty of use of during the test.

Firing up the familiar, smooth yet strong 2.6-litre six, I had a sudden pang of trepidation; would this 276bhp(ish) un-tuned classic feel a bit Godzouki rather than Godzilla? After all, I hadn't owned a car with much less than 400 horsepower for the past seven years, and the last R32 I drove was Tim Milne's fearsome 600+bhp 2.8-litre beast (Track Shootout, **evo** 24).

The first squeeze of the throttle dispelled that thought immediately as a thrilling wave of mid-range torque pushed my back into the seat. What was even more surprising was that the thrust continued, in fact increased, right up to our self-imposed 7000rpm limit. This propensity to rev could be due partially to the freer-breathing Trust exhaust system, but the fact remains that this is still a seriously fast car.

On torrentially wet roads this Skyline had no problem breaking traction, both from rest and all the way around corners. In most other cars that

R32 leads the pack, looking almost lithe and subtle compared to brawnier, heavier R33 and positively brutal R34 in the background

'It just feels like a perfectly balanced rear-wheel-drive car with uncanny traction'

might have been a worry, but in a GT-R it's merely the cue to keep your toe in and have fun.

On entering a bend, the Super-HICAS four-wheel-steer system resists understeer by steering the rear wheels initially in the opposite direction to the fronts, then latterly in parallel to help stabilise the car when it's settled into the corner. But the ATTESSA electronic torque split only diverts power to the front wheels when the rears slip, hence the need to keep power applied so the fronts can help to pull the car out of the slide.

This is the point where sceptics say, 'where's the fun if the car does it all for you?' Answer is, it doesn't. You still have to apply the right amount

of opposite lock at the right time and wind it off at the correct rate too, as well as re-learning how to use the throttle as described.

But forget how the R32 GT-R does what it does; how does it *feel* when it's doing it? In a word, fan-bloody-tastic! There's never been a better power-assisted steering system for feel and feedback than this one. Every nuance of grip and road surface is conveyed subtly and accurately through the rim and the slight initial understeer is telegraphed clearly, telling you that lateral grip limits have been exceeded. Provided the exit to the corner is clear, a slight squeeze of the throttle sends the tail out in classic front-

HISTORY OF THE GT-R

Most westerners don't appreciate that the Skyline GT-R has a history to rival the Porsche 911. The first Skyline was made by Prince Motors (then soon to be taken over by Nissan) as long ago as 1957, though only as a four-door family saloon.

By the time the third generation came out in 1968, Nissan had decided to enter Japanese touring car racing and in February 1969 released the PGC 10, known as the 2000 GT-R. Built specially for racing, using a 2-litre straight six producing 160bhp (equivalent to the 911 of the day), this four-door saloon first raced in May 1969. Halfway through its life production switched to the more attractive KPGC 10 coupe (below). Between them, the saloon and coupe took 50 race victories.

The fourth-generation Skyline arrived in 1972 and the 2000 GT-R name lived on as a four-door saloon or two-door coupe. However, when production ceased in '77, the GT-R badge disappeared.

In 1989 the R32 Skyline GT-R was launched with a mission to dominate Group A touring car racing, which it did, worldwide.

Even in filthy weather like this, the R33 won't lose its grip. Its storming yet serene ground-covering ability is as breathtaking now as it always was

R32 GT-R (above and bottom right) is massive fun in the wet. R34 V-spec (right) quicker but demands more concentration

...ngined rear-drive fashion, but the way to gather ...in is to counter-steer and give the throttle even ...ore pressure. This transforms powerslides from ...lly, speed-wasting indulgence to, within reason, ...e fastest way to accelerate out of a corner.

The R32 does all this with the highest level of ...volvement; you are totally unaware of the ...chnology, apart from the fact you are grinning ...om ear to ear and accelerating away from ...orners that would be a sweat-soaked nightmare ...lesser vehicles. It just feels like a perfectly ...alanced rear-wheel-drive car with uncanny ...action. Unlikely as it sounds, this car feels pure. ...fact the only R32 weakspot is the brakes. By ...odern standards they're appalling.

On to the R33. This one, like my late lamented ...odzilla, is a V-spec ('V' is for victory, originally ...en on a special-edition R32 celebrating three ...ears of continuous victories in Group A racing), ...hich means it features a computer-controlled ...tive rear LSD that can apportion torque side-...-side to further control the cornering attitude ...f the car. R33 V-specs also have firmer, lower ...spension than their vanilla GT-R brethren. ...Matt Osborne's dark metallic grey example has ...one more than the average mileage for a 1997 ...odel but, like Dave's 13-year-old R32, still feels ...ght and rattle-free. Although still strong in ...solute terms, this totally standard car felt ...oticeably less gutsy than the R32, particularly ...ward the top end. This could be due partly to ...e older car's sports exhaust, but probably has ...ore to do with the extra weight the 33 carries. ...With wider tyres (245 section, 17in items ...rsus the 225, 16in covers on the 32) the R33 ...as loads more grip on the drenched tarmac. ...ll throttle in first gear fails to excite the rear ...res in a straight line and stability through ...anding water is exceptional. On a tight and ...isty B-road, a well-driven Evo VI might be ...ightly faster, but nothing can match the serene ...ay in which this car copes with wet conditions. ...You're kept very well informed about what is ...oing on, both through the seat and the wheel, ...t with better tyres, a longer wheelbase and the ...tra layer of electronics, it's always under ...ontrol. Even the tightest second-gear bends ...n't allow sideways shenanigans, at least not on ...blic roads. This car is staggeringly competent, ...t surprisingly different from its predecessor. ...Finally it's time to try Cem Kocu's Bayside ...ue R34 GT-R V-spec. On the R34, V-spec not ...ly means stiffer suspension and the active rear ...SD, but also a deeper front spoiler and carbon ...ar diffuser as well as more functions on the ...onderful Multi Function Display that replaces ...me of the earlier models' dials. ...Biggest initial differences are that the steering

	R32 GT-R	R33 GT-R V-SPEC	R34 GT-R V-SPEC
○ Engine	In-line six, 2568cc, 24v, twin turbo	In-line six, 2568cc, 24v, twin turbo	In-line six, 2568cc, 24v, twin turbo
● Max power	276bhp @ 6800rpm	276bhp @ 6800rpm	276bhp @ 7000rpm
● Max torque	260lb ft @ 4400rpm	271lb ft @ 4400rpm	289lb ft @ 4400rpm
○ Weight (kerb)	1480kg	1540kg	1560kg
○ Power-to-weight	189bhp/ton	182bhp/ton	180bhp/ton
○ 0-60mph	5.2sec	5.4sec	4.7sec
○ Top speed	155mph	155mph	165mph
evo RATING	★★★★ 1/2	★★★★	★★★★

is heavier, despite having the same width tyres (on 18in rims), and that there are now six gears. The engine feels stronger than the R33, although again, Cem's car has a sports exhaust, in this case a factory-fitted Nismo system.

The suspension is noticeably harder than the R33 V-spec's and introduces an element of 'hopping' over small bumps and undulations that simply isn't there in the other two cars. This bounciness, coupled with fairly severe tramlining means that, unlike the earlier cars, punting the 34 at speed along wet B-roads requires a firm grip on the wheel and maximum concentration.

The second-gear corner that was delirious, drifting fun in the 32 and completely safe in the 33, allows a small amount of tail-out action in the 34, but at much higher speed than in the 32.

On smoother A-roads, the R34 is devastatingly effective with extremely direct steering, excellent brakes, rifle-bolt action close-ratio gearbox and a characterful, zesty engine that is noticeably more powerful at the top end. For track use, this would definitely be

the most effective weapon of the three.

But for the road, which one would I have? Judging purely on fun factor, it would have to be the R32. Oh, and I forgot to mention that Dave paid a mere £10,000 for his car, only a few months ago. Sometimes, the original is best. ■

Thanks to Dave Redpath, Matt Osborne, Cem Kocu and the GT-R Register for their help with this feature.

STORY **CHRIS HARRIS** PHOTOGRAPHS **ALEX PUCZYNIEC**

THE FAST & THE FURIOUS

Mid-engined supercar takes on high-tech trickery four-wheel-driver. Classic facelifted NSX versus turbo-nutter Skyline. A clash that settles a few scores

The Honda NSX pre-dates my professional relationship with the motor car. As recently as last year everything I knew about it was based on the opinions of my predecessors, and a fair few of my current colleagues.

If Japan's first genuine supercar was a fascinating thing to read about, then it must have been a deeply engaging subject to scribble about. The backdrop was perfect: Japan was rapidly emerging as a maker of quality product, and Honda's

supremacy in Formula One and the official assistance of a certain A Senna in honing the finished article lent it enormous credibility. Hacks twitched with excitement while Ferrari's 348 twitched with fear (and more than a little lift-off oversteer).

Beyond my ken, I'm afraid. Didn't know the fella, having had a quick steer of one late in 2001 and being left perfectly unimpressed. You see Harris's Japanese performance fantasies are inextricably linked to a different breed, one fondly known at fortress *Autocar* as the

turbo-nutter era. A gene-pool that has given us some of the most exciting road cars ever and a bucket full of the finest names – Nissan Skyline GT-R, Mitsubishi Evo, Impreza STi. For the purposes of this particular investigation, it was a type of car that made us forget all about the Honda NSX.

For a generation of *Gran Turismo* addicts like me, the Honda that once shamed its equivalent Ferrari was nothing more than an expensive and tricky handling side-show that got in the way of the game's juicier offerings. It's not ◗

RE02 KNO

127

Harsh ride of GT-R
makes it an unfriendly
multi-lane tool; NSX is
firm but compliant

◆ just that we didn't believe the hype, we hadn't even heard it. Far-eastern performance parlance was all hissing overboost and four driven Bridgestones.

Well, now Japan's prototypical supercar has returned all lean and frisky – and at a £10,000 leaner price of £59,995, too – to whisper quietly in the ear of its onetime nemesis: the Skyline GT-R. It was the Nissan that first shifted the focus away from Honda's pure, mid-engined, rear-wheel driver.

Mild cosmetic tweaks to the Honda include, at last, decent headlights and a fresh set of bumpers. But that devilishly long rear end remains, and so do the overall proportions. Most important, though, it still looks elegant; unmistakably NSX. Considerably sleeker than its opponent here, the current £54,000 R34 Skyline GT-R.

Right now, the big Nissan looks like it has all the delicacy of a bull-mastiff in a greyhound race; upright, long and forcing that trademark gob at the world. Looks surprisingly old, too: there's no doubting that the previous generation R33 has worn its years with more dignity.

Honda has embraced the improvement philosophy pioneered by Porsche during the late '70s and '80s for the 911: do nothing much, but if you actually do something, make it look right. Which means that beyond its facial nip and tuck, the NSX is largely the same car. Spring rates are stiffer at the front, the rear anti-roll bar is marginally larger, and the rear track is forced out another 10mm to work with larger 245/40 ZR17 tyres.

But the same 3179cc V6 sits longitudinally between the axles and produces a claimed 276bhp at 7300rpm and 224lb ft of torque at 5300rpm. As we'll find later, that word 'claimed' is of considerable significance.

The Skyline registers the same 276bhp on the dyno, this time at 6800rpm but pummels the Honda for torque, deploying a full 293lb ft at 4400rpm through its computer controlled four-wheel drive.

Good news for Mr NSX, there's not a sniff of rain as we wander past Bristol, over the green bridge and on to some of Europe's finest roads. Glad to be perched where I am, too, snug in the NSX's leather chair, peering out over the lightly raised wing tops with legs pretty much extended straight out in front. As driving positions go it isn't perfect – the wheel is always set too low – but it still feels pretty special.

Rides nicely, too. Ignores the isolation game played by luxo-saloons and in the search for ultimate body control it's prepared to acknowledge every blister on the road's surface. But does so with good manners; it never crashes or thumps too hard into stuff and adds a genuine GT edge to the curriculum vitae. I'm impressed already.

And thankful not to be in the Nissan. Japan's firmest-riding export has long been a motorway torture tool, but worse than I recall when I finally do switch. The ride is impossibly hard – no, that's untrue, it doesn't ride at all. Even the smallest pits shimmy through the body structure and, worse still, the R34's addiction to camber changes is more marked than I remember. At least the seat's gripping me in just the right places, and the wheel/pedal relationship is ideal. But even on crisp, new motorway the car bugs you with dialogue you're just not interested in. Pegging a GT-R back to a sensible UK cruise has always been a cruel exercise, though.

And it's one to be forgotten about the moment we peel northwards off the M4 and leave monotony behind. I'm still in the Nissan when we begin to explore some bigger dash numbers; the Skyline's doing a decent job of rectifying the dam-

"THE BIG NISSAN LOOKS LIKE IT HAS ALL THE DELICACY OF A BULL-MASTIFF IN A GREYHOUND RACE"

NSX cabin over a decade old, largely unchanged, still works well; comfortable

GT-R cabin doesn't feel as classy despite Connolly leather; boy racer techno gimmicks

age it did to my spine an hour earlier. Unrelenting firmness at a cruise translates into race-car body control on a sumptuous mix of A- and B-roads. Cambers are an issue, however, especially under braking, and the Skyline's 245/40 ZR 18 Bridgestones prefer to ignore alterations in the road surface when it's loaded up with the full 1605kg. Absorption isn't a concept it likes to do business with, and that ultimately limits the car's cross-country ability in the UK.

Fast though. Gather 3000rpm together, get the electronic boost needle wagging, and this is still a breathtaking method of gathering speed. Rest to 60mph is a 4.6sec thump in the back and you tackle motorway slip roads safe in the knowledge that anything capable of a standing ton in 10.8sec is not to be toyed with unless you're suitably equipped. By that I mean 911 Turbo-style.

But it's the Nissan engineers' take on four-wheel drive that sets it apart from anything else. This should be a chassis configuration which promotes grip and traction; designed to eliminate both under and oversteer and generally rid ▶

The Porsche 911 factor

Entry to this contest was restricted to those with a Japanese passport, so the 911 wasn't invited. To compensate, therefore, we took a quick trip to Wales in the basic Carrera 2 – one of the most impressive sports cars ever – that scored full marks in a supercar test in our Christmas double issue.

Fixed buckets and no rear seats drop the 911 nicely into NSX territory, and similarities between the two cars on Welsh roads are quite clear. Both have that unique brand of tight but supple body control ideal for such territory, and the performance needed to sprint between them. Raw ability is matched by sheer speed; these are the kind of roads where an Impreza feels no swifter than a 1.8 Mondeo and would be demolished by either of our two lead Japanese players and the 911.

To be honest, I expected this contest to pan out into an all-Japanese knuckle fight, with the 911 waiting patiently to deflate the eventual winner. Well, the NSX quickly won the domestic scrap, but then proceeded to sink its teeth into the 911. The notebook doesn't lie, and it reads: the NSX has slightly tighter body control at speed than the Porsche and as good a ride. Better-sounding engine at high revs; shorter,

crisper shift. The 911 counters with stronger brakes and less fade, far crisper steering, more torque out of bends, a more adjustable line with the right foot.

Too close to call? Almost. Then you factor in the everyday appeal of the Porsche, the extra performance (0-100mph in 10.1sec) and its practicality and it just gets the nod. But only just.

911 one of the best ever: steering in a class of one

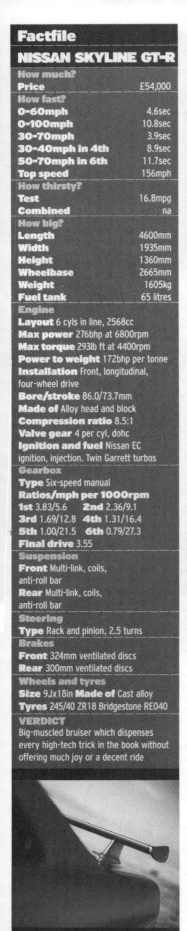

Factfile
NISSAN SKYLINE GT-R

How much?	
Price	£54,000

How fast?	
0-60mph	4.6sec
0-100mph	10.8sec
30-70mph	3.9sec
30-40mph in 4th	8.9sec
50-70mph in 6th	11.7sec
Top speed	156mph

How thirsty?	
Test	16.8mpg
Combined	na

How big?	
Length	4600mm
Width	1935mm
Height	1360mm
Wheelbase	2665mm
Weight	1605kg
Fuel tank	65 litres

Engine
Layout 6 cyls in line, 2568cc
Max power 276bhp at 6800rpm
Max torque 293lb ft at 4400rpm
Power to weight 172bhp per tonne
Installation Front, longitudinal, four-wheel drive
Bore/stroke 86.0/73.7mm
Made of Alloy head and block
Compression ratio 8.5:1
Valve gear 4 per cyl, dohc
Ignition and fuel Nissan EC ignition, injection. Twin Garrett turbos

Gearbox
Type Six-speed manual

Ratios/mph per 1000rpm			
1st	3.83/5.6	2nd	2.36/9.1
3rd	1.69/12.8	4th	1.31/16.4
5th	1.00/21.5	6th	0.79/27.3
Final drive 3.55			

Suspension
Front Multi-link, coils, anti-roll bar
Rear Multi-link, coils, anti-roll bar

Steering
Type Rack and pinion, 2.5 turns

Brakes
Front 324mm ventilated discs
Rear 300mm ventilated discs

Wheels and tyres
Size 9Jx18in **Made of** Cast alloy
Tyres 245/40 ZR18 Bridgestone RE040

VERDICT
Big-muscled bruiser which dispenses every high-tech trick in the book without offering much joy or a decent ride

Honda's glorious V6 has advantage of always being on song, unlike laggy Nissan's

GT-R a four-wheel driver, but it has rear-drive manners

V.spec

the world of sideways motoring. Hardly a pilgrimage of note, but useful stuff in a forest if your name's McRae.

Yet the four-wheel-drive Skyline plays Hooligan longer and harder than just about any other car on sale. Because it's a rear-driver in drag. Yes, I can't deny the existence of a couple of front drive-shafts, but it's best to disregard them and use the GT-R as a power-oversteer tool.

Here's why: full boost, second gear corner and you're on the gas nice and early. Not a sniff of understeer. Oh no. Instead an instant step into that delicious world where the back wheels desperately want to corner faster than their friends up front: oversteer. Heaps of it and well before the apex of the bend. In with the opposite lock, and then the clever HICAS brain begins to blend in front-driven traction to get things moving forward. That first sideways Skyline experience is unforgettable for its sheer controllability . Looks damned heroic, too.

Such a taste for the good stuff does hamper the GT-R in other, more real world, situations though. A big old boat, it doesn't do a great job of hiding its girth. Steers accurately enough, but desperately wants you to prod the throttle a little too hard, just so it can show off its corrective magic, and that robs it of the fluency truly great road cars summon up to string corners together. A fluency the NSX is just about to teach the young pup all about.

I adore defining moments: first times, last times. The dawnings of truth, of clarity. The NSX delivered one such event for me, which is astonishing given that it has

been knocking about for over a decade. I've shamelessly subscribed to the Evo-nutter generation for years and yet the NSX is about to dismantle, systematically, the Skyline's reputation over what should be a perfect Skyline road. Think I'm about to chuck in my membership.

Because the NSX is quite simply a superior means of covering ground promptly and – this is the really hurtful bit for the Skyline – enjoyably.

It all starts with that exceptional V6. Still displacing 3.2 litres and boasting a claimed output that a BMW saloon would laugh at, Honda has somehow

"THE NSX DRIVETRAIN IS IS SENSATIONAL, ONE THAT STANDS COMPARISON WITH ITALY'S BEST"

A delicate handler; grippy, balanced, but steering isn't perfect

Nissan invites oversteer just to prove how controllable it is

Factfile
HONDA NSX

How much?	
Price	£59,995
How fast?	
0-60mph	4.8sec
0-100mph	10.9sec
30-70mph	4.0sec
30-40mph in 4th	4.6sec
50-70mph in 6th	8.0sec
Top speed	172mph
How thirsty?	
Test	21.0mpg
Combined	22.8mpg
How big?	
Length	4430mm
Width	1810mm
Height	1160mm
Wheelbase	2530mm
Weight	1320kg
Fuel tank	70 litres

Engine
Layout 6 cyls in vee, 3179cc
Max power 276bhp at 7300rpm
Max torque 224lb ft at 5300rpm
Power to weight 209bhp per tonne
Installation Mid, longitudinal, rear-wheel drive
Bore/stroke 93.0/78.0mm
Made of Alloy heads and block
Compression ratio 10.2:1
Valve gear 4 per cyl, dohc per bank
Ignition and fuel PGM-F1 programmed fuel injection, VTEC
Gearbox
Type Six-speed manual
Ratios/mph per 1000rpm
1st 3.06/5.7   **2nd** 1.95/9.0
3rd 1.43/12.3   **4th** 1.12/15.6
5th 0.91/19.2   **6th** 0.72/24.5
Final drive 4.10
Suspension
Front and rear Double wishbones, coils, anti-roll bar
Steering
Type Rack and pinion, 3.1 turns
Brakes
Front 298mm ventilated discs
Rear 303mm ventilated discs
Wheels and tyres
Size 7.5Jx17 (f), 8.5Jx18in (r)
Made of Cast alloy
Tyres 215/45 ZR17 (f), 245/40 ZR18 (r)
VERDICT
Reinvigorated decade-old supercar has it all: a fine ride, glorious and tractable engine, terrific punch, superb balance

managed to coax nearly a second out of the claimed standing-quarter-mile time. The car's no lighter than before and the way time itself passes hasn't altered radically over the past four years, so it's fair to assume that the NSX has been telling porkies in the dyno room. This gentleman's 276bhp agreement is looking sillier by the day.

It's a sensational drivetrain: one that draws and stands comparison with the very best efforts from Italy. A decade's worth of engine management nous has made the NSX's low-speed manners seem quite ordinary; it's anything but when you open the throttles wide, though. Then it's all induction noise; a gorgeous stream from just behind the passenger's head, and one that builds with the power delivery until an 8000rpm cut off. You extend it just for the thrill.

It feels massively quick, too. At least as fast as the Skyline when it's on full boost; and when driven in convoy, it's easily the

faster of the pair, especially when the GT-R's turbo is caught napping, as it often is. The urge is much more than subjective and the inlet bark is plenty justified by a 4.8sec 0-60mph run and 10.9sec 0-100mph sprint. In fact, this car is so much quicker, so much more urgent at any speed in any gear, than the previous NSX, it deserves a different name. No engine modifications, my foot.

But once again the electrically assisted steering is a let down. Well judged for speed just off centre and not exactly poorly weighted, the wheel still doesn't involve you in the way it should. Load it up mid corner and it becomes leaden, unresponsive and decidedly unreassuring. But work through the system's odd dead points and this is a supremely agile car; one that changes direction far better than the Skyline and, for all the rack's faults, is easier to place. Grip is keener, too, and it's capable of working into the muscle of those new 298mm (front) and

303mm (rear) discs with real enthusiasm. There's so much reassurance in the movement of the middle pedal and the quality of the retardation on tap, that you find yourself attacking braking areas. Then finding grip and playing with the car's attitude on the throttle; not big steering angles like the GT-R's, but smaller, defter inputs that are more satisfying.

The upshot's simple. Old-school NSX gives the brash youngster a good whooping over these roads. Gives it a sound beating in any circumstances come to think of it. Immeasurably more chilled a device in which to cruise, better to sit in and more carefully assembled: it's a crushing victory and one I just didn't expect. The Skyline still has the odd trick up its sleeve, but it's feeling old in this company. The NSX remains an exemplary piece of precision engineering, honed into a fine driving experience; one whose qualities have outlasted a generation of less well-conceived rivals. ●

It's called the Forest of Bowland, but there aren't many trees. In the heart of Lancashire's upland country, this stark and beautiful moorland is within 20 miles of (but a world away from) the pigeon-fanciers and cobbled streets of the caricature North West. Near the top of Catlow Fell, only the warbling birds, wind-tousled grass and the occasional RAF jet disturb the peace. Miles of sinuous tarmac, whose gritty surface is barely worn, twist, climb and plunge their way through valleys and over peaks, sprawling like a loosely-woven net to connect remote farms and timeworn rustic cottages with civilisation. This is wild terrain, and it's prime Skyline GT-R territory.

Forget, if you will, that Nissan developed this car for the track. The R32 Skyline GT-R (to give it its full name) was designed to beat the BMW E30 M3 and the Ford Sierra RS Cosworth in international Group A racing, but its unique blend of toughness and technology (and there's lots of that) makes it a formidable road car.

Every part of the Skyline – bodyshell, engine, steering, suspension, drivetrain – that could possibly affect the way it handles was optimised to extraordinary lengths by obsessive Japanese engineers, intent on obliterating the competition. Given the chance to unleash one when launched at the Nürburgring's Nordschleife in 1989, *Car* magazine dubbed it 'the world's most advanced road

car'. More than a decade (and two generations) on, that same technology underpins the current R34 GT-R, and the car that kick-started it all can be yours for the price of an ordinary new hatchback. The moorland roads are calling.

WHAT STRIKES you first is the GT-R's sheer solidity. I'm not talking muffled door thunks and precision-action indicator stalks; rather the kind of billet-like heft that instils confidence as soon as you clamp yourself into the driving seat and grip the fat leather-rimmed wheel. You feel it through the steering column, the gearlever, and through the structure as you pull away. There isn't a spare ounce to the GT-R, but it feels tense and muscle-bound, as focused as a racing greyhound waiting for the gate to drop.

What you don't immediately sense is the stack of technology, there with the sole purpose of extracting milliseconds from lap times.

Open the bonnet and there, stuffed in so tight they had to cant it at an angle, is a 2.6-litre, 24-valve, twin-cam, twin-turbocharged straight six. Those turbos employ ceramic turbines for better heat resistance and run in ball bearings, cutting friction by half compared to conventional units, all of which makes for quicker reactions and reduced lag. Thanks to a gentleman's agreement among Japanese manufacturers, power output is officially rated at 276bhp, but rumours spread by Nissan engineers

When Nissan launched the R32 Skyline GT-R, it made a bid to out-Porsche Porsche. In so doing, it created the world's most advanced road car. We drive it
Words: Glen Waddington
Photography: Michael Baillie

Reach for the sky

suggest a true 300bhp. That's a specific output of 115bhp per litre, more than a modern Ferrari 360 Modena, and it's just a taster for a technical spec-list that could have come from an Eighties sci-fi movie.

Most amazingly, there's four-wheel steering. The rears turn through a maximum of just one degree, but they counter-steer first for sharper turn-in, and then move in phase with the fronts for stability. The computer sorts the maths out and electro-hydraulics take care of the movement.

Then there's four-wheel drive. Unlike Audi's Quattro system, it's not permanent, but don't expect some half-cocked lever-selected operation. The GT-R only sends drive to the front wheels when its sensors and computers decide to, so you get the cornering security of four-wheel drive without the potential understeer of a constant torque-feed.

Even the legendary Porsche 959 scrabbles away 20 per cent of its power through the front wheels at the limit. As one of Nissan's engineers told *Car* at the Nürburgring: 'Porsche makes the best-handling cars and the 959 is the most advanced supercar ever made. We wanted to beat the 959.' Nothing has truly outsmarted the GT-R since. Even the successive R33 and R34 are refinements of the R32.

Not surprisingly, Nissan dreamed up a couple of acronyms for the gizmology. So, we have ATTESA E-TS (Advanced Total Traction Engineering System for All terrains, with Electronic Torque Split), otherwise known as four-wheel drive. And the tricky steering is Super HICAS (Hi Capacity Actively Steers).

Thankfully, and unlike many other Eighties Japanese performance cars, Nissan chose not to emblazon techno-babble all over the GT-R. Instead, all is cool understatement. The Skyline coupé (there was a four-door saloon, too) is a simple shape, one that evolved from previous Skyline generations (R32 is the eighth) and on to today's R34. There to proclaim its venomous intentions are ground-scraping stance, sinister dark grey alloy wheels, bulging wheelarches, air-dam and wing spoiler. In wet weather, you can see the spoiler in action, channeling rain in swirling patterns as it goes about its aerodynamic business.

Raising a giggle rather than derision are the afterthought attempts at cod heritage: a Seventies-looking 'lightning strike' S (for Skyline) badge to the nose and cheesy GT-R badges that look like accessory shop add-ons for a souped-up Cortina. The heritage is real, though. Skylines have been around for more than 40 years, and from 1969 to 1977 you could buy a GT-R looking like a tin-plate Mustang. About as advanced too, with their cart-sprung live rear axles.

When the R32 revived the mantle in 1989, there was no laughter. Desperate to shake off the dowdy days of the Cherry and Bluebird, Nissan went racing and was so successful that Group A banned the works GT-R. Undeterred, it took the Primera saloon touring car racing and fed its track expertise straight back to the road cars. Nissan has slowly won a reputation for great drivers' cars (even though they don't look it), and the GT-R has been its technical showcase ever since.

TO SHAKE OFF THE CHERRY AND BLUEBIRD, NISSAN WENT RACING AND WAS SO SUCCESSFUL THAT GROUP A BANNED THE WORKS GT-R

I WATCH the GT-R thunder across the Lancashire moorland, as owner Brian McKenzie performs for the camera. The muted bellow of its exhaust combines with the whistle of the twin-turbos, imitating the jets overhead, and the circular brake lights glow like afterburners when he pulls up.

Then it's my turn. Even at a standstill, you sense awesome potency. That straight six idles with a throb that you feel as much as hear. Selecting first gear with a steely 'dink-dink' through the closely-defined gate, you raise the revs, release the clutch, and there's an almost imperceptible thunk through the driveline as the throb smooths to a jet-like whoosh. You're off, with perfect traction to guarantee the perfect getaway. With so much power, it's a quick one, too.

After take-off, the fighter-plane analogy transforms into something more animalistic. The GT-R is a lion chasing zebras across the grassy African plains of the Masai Mara. It darts and weaves, clawing its course as the front wheels dig in and drag the rears into shape, while a stampede of roaring engine and the thump and thud of suspension through the rigid bodyshell assaults your eardrums. It sounds dramatic, and it'll have you grinning like a madman, yet it's all so easy. The GT-R is a raw and communicative drive, but it's fundamentally refined; aggressive but also poised and contained like a big cat going in for the kill.

No car with this potential has a right to be so undemanding. Think about it. Nissan built the GT-R to annihilate competition on the track, yet here you are with 300bhp attacking challenging roads as if it's the sort of thing everybody does before breakfast. It's one of those cars that just feels right, from the way the driving seat grips you, to your position behind the wheel, and the consistent weighting and linear response of all the major controls.

It's a big car that doesn't feel it. The Skyline sits in Nissan's Japanese market hierarchy roughly where the Granada sat in Ford's, yet it feels nimble like a Lancia Delta Integrale. Enter a corner at a speed that seems too fast (and it will, at first) and you have to make a mental readjustment to power on in and through. Back off, and you'll be sideways into the scenery just like any other powerful rear-wheel drive car. But keep the power on and the brakes' ABS sensors realise that the rear tyres are beyond the limits of grip. Only then is torque transmitted to the front axle, where it plunders the available traction and pulls you through. There's even a little gauge on the dash to tell you what it's doing.

Steering is pure and kart-like, the messages between tarmac and palm unmuddied by the electronics. You only realise it's power assisted because it's never too heavy, and the rear wheel steering is intuitive rather than alien. Turn in, and

Twin-turbo, 24-valve, twin-cam, straight six said to be good for 300bhp; it's more of a supercar than its understated styling suggests

1992 NISSAN R32 SKYLINE GT-R

Engine
Six-cylinder, dohc, 24-valve, 2568cc, twin-turbocharged, electronic fuel injection
Power and torque
276bhp @ 6800rpm
260lb ft @ 4400rpm
Transmission
Five-speed manual, four-wheel drive
Brakes
Ventilated discs all round, ABS
Suspension
Front: independent, multi-link wishbones, coil springs,

telescopic dampers, anti-roll bar Rear: independent, multi-link wishbones, coil springs, telescopic dampers, electronic steering
Weight
3153lb (1430kg)
Performance
Top speed: 156mph
0-60mph: 5.6sec (*Guinness World Car Records*)
Cost new
£20,000 approx (in Japan)
Value now
£20,000-25,000

the rear tyres step out just a fraction, to pivot the car about the driving seat. You feel like Tazio Nuvolari.

Of course, it's fast. Put your foot down in any gear and the instantaneous pick-up swiftly burgeons a hundredfold as the turbos spool to full strength and catapult you toward the horizon. You can play racing drivers, whipping through the gears to the accompaniment of a seismic soundtrack that flourishes to a muted scream, for all the world like a Porsche 911 with the bass turned up and the treble turned down. Or surf a wave of torque, relax, and relish a firm, flat, tied-down ride. Raw sports car or refined GT? The choice is yours.

Fellow Oriental sports cars like the Mitsubishi 3000GT proved that too much technology can get in the way and take the life out of driving, but in the GT-R it's as if it isn't there. The straightforward bits are ingenious, like the double wishbone suspension all round with additional links to make for perfect geometry. Aluminium front wings and bonnet make for a kerbweight of 1430kg, barely 100kg more than the smaller, less complex Porsche 944S2. And the interior is just like the exterior: understated, utilitarian, focused rather than glamorous. It wouldn't hurt to rip it apart, fit a roll cage, and go racing.

It's easy to imagine Japanese engineers curtly inputting information into computers, crunching the numbers and turning theory into reality. Yet the GT-R is evidence of human warmth. It feels like Nissan's

men swapped lab coats for rally jackets and pounded the product until they were proud of the result.

RARELY IS reality more incredible than the hype, but I think I've found an answer to the perennial question: 'If you could have any car, but only that car, what would it be?' The R32 GT-R is the ultimate multi-purpose classic.

It's got competition heritage but shopping car reliability. It does all the hairshirt sports car things a 911 will, yet it never threatens to bite back. Maybe the badge lacks prestige, but R32 is a cult all its own, recognised only by a discerning cognoscenti. Hell, it's even got four seats and a boot.

Unlike later GT-Rs, it was never officially imported into Britain, and there are only about 70 here, yet find a decent one and it should set you back no more than £15,000. Back home in Japan, good R32s fetch more than R33s – as so often, original is best, and successive models have got heavier and harsher.

The R32 GT-R is a car of genuine integrity, designed to do a job which it did so perfectly it got banned. Everything Nissan did to win on the track just happens to make for an awe-inspiring road car. No manufacturer, not even Nissan, has bettered it.

Thanks to: Brian McKenzie for his superb Skyline; Middlehurst Motorsport (01744 26681); Datsun Owners' Club: contact William Lightburn on 01342 321000.

AN EXPERT'S VIEW

ANDY Middlehurst runs Middlehurst Motorsport in St Helens, Lancs, the only dealership officially sanctioned by Nissan to sell the R34 Skyline GT-R. He won the 1995-96 Group N touring car championship overall in his R32 GT-R, with 16 outright victories in two years, despite being forced to carry a 110kg leadweight handicap!

He says: 'Treat an R32 GT-R with respect and it will be incredibly reliable – one of my customer's cars is still going strong with 150,000 miles on the clock. Regular expert maintenance is key. However, the youngest are nearly ten years old, and parts are expensive. It's an easy car to tune – a new engine management chip and increased boost pressure will see an easy 440bhp, but the ceramic turbines can shatter in extremes, and an engine rebuild costs £3000.

'The R32 is lighter and more nimble than later models, and is highly sought after in Japan. Problem is, cars are cheaper there, and treated with less respect. They're often

very highly tuned, at the expense of longevity, so it makes sense to source one in Britain although they're rare here: typically worth £10,000-15,000, with mint examples at around £20,000.'

Andy Middlehurst on the track, in his racing R32 Skyline GT-R

AN HISTORIC VIEW

THERE'S been a Skyline in Nissan's line-up since Nissan merged with fellow Japanese manufacturer Prince in 1966. But the Skyline itself goes back to 1957, and its competition history to 1965, when Prince first entered the car in Japanese saloon car racing.

Says Nigel Gates, Skyline expert at the Datsun Owners' Club: 'The mid-Sixties Skyline GT-A and GT-B have the sort of respect in Japan that the Lotus Cortina has in Britain. Prince was a very technically-minded company, and Nissan kept its spirit alive with the Skyline.

'In 1969, the third generation Skyline arrived, and with it the GT-R badge. That car dominated Japanese saloon car racing before Mazda came along with the RX-3. It had a 2.0-litre, twin-cam, 24-valve, triple-carb straight six, good for 160bhp. Good short-wheelbase coupé versions fetch £20,000 in Japan.'

With the fourth generation in 1972, the GT-R became more of a road car; the fuel crisis put paid to the GT-R in 1977. Nissan's philosophy had changed, and the big Skyline coupé became more of a luxury cruiser. It found its sporting feet again in 1981, with the 190bhp four-cylinder R30 RS Turbo, and in 1986, the R31 GTS-X

went back to the Skyline's twin-cam six-cylinder roots but provided a foretaste of the R32, with four-wheel steering.

Says Nigel: 'Nissan got the taste for racing again, and laid down the gauntlet in the technology stakes. When the R32 revived the GT-R name in 1989, it was so far ahead of its time that they've hardly altered it since.'

Nissan Skyline GT-R arrived in 1969 as a four-door saloon

First GT-R engine was a 160bhp, 2.0-litre, triple-carb, straight six